THE NOVEL CORONAVIRUS ORIGINATED IN CHINA:

LESSONS FOR HUMANKIND

SPIRITUAL MESSAGES FROM SHIBASABURO KITASATO AND R. A. GOAL

RYUHO OKAWA

HS PRESS

The opinions of the spirit and space being in this book do not necessarily reflect those of Happy Science Group.
For the mechanism behind spiritual messages, see the end section.

Contents

PART ONE

The Truth behind the Virus War Started by China

CHAPTER ONE

Spiritual Messages from Shibasaburo Kitasato

CHAPTER TWO

Analysis of the Future from Space

-Spiritual Messages from R. A. Goal-

PART TWO

Messages from R. A. Goal

CHAPTER ONE

Warnings of the Pro-China Mentality

-Spiritual Messages from R. A. Goal-

CHAPTER TWO

Talking about
the Savior on a Cosmic Scale
beyond the Earth

-UFO Reading 46 (R. A. Goal)-

Preface

Please just read this book first.

This collection contains a spiritual message from Shibasaburo Kitasato, who once made achievements in measures against infectious diseases, and spiritual communications from R. A. Goal, a space being whose name has appeared even in *The New York Times*, asking about the present and future of the novel coronavirus infection that originated in China, which is rapidly spreading all over the world.

As the information changes day by day, it is extremely difficult to explore the root cause and predict the future, but even if conventional "common sense believers" insult, abuse, condemn, or criticize me, I must say what I must. This is my holy mission.

Although there are rules that say space people cannot usually intervene in the Earth civilization, it has been said that they can intervene when humankind is in a crisis and when the Earth civilization is about to be destroyed. Then, maybe, "Now is the time."

Some of the gods in ancient myths are not of Earth origin. Let's be humble and listen to what they have to say.

Ryuho Okawa
Master & CEO of Happy Science Group
April 21, 2020

PART ONE

The Truth behind
the Virus War Started by China

The situation when Part One was recorded

The state of coronavirus infections as of March 30, 2020, the day the two spiritual messages in Part One were recorded, was 786,804 infected and 38,581 dead in the world. The numbers in Japan were 1,953 infected and 56 dead. Mr. Xi Jinping's visit to Japan as a state guest and the Tokyo Olympics had already been postponed. However, Japan was still carefully considering whether or not to declare a nationwide state of emergency.

CHAPTER ONE

Spiritual Messages from Shibasaburo Kitasato

Originally recorded in Japanese on March 30, 2020,
in the Special Lecture Hall of Happy Science in Japan,
and later translated into English.

Shibasaburo Kitasato (1853 - 1931)

Bacteriologist. Kitasato studied under Robert Koch in Germany in 1886, then succeeded in developing a pure culture of tetanus bacteria as well as serum therapy in 1889. After returning to Japan, he served as the director of the Institute of Infectious Diseases. Kitasato contributed to the development of public health and medicine, including the discovery of the plague bacillus and the prevention of tuberculosis.

In this book, the interviewer will be abbreviated as A.

1

A Surprise Move by China Regarding the Novel Coronavirus

Summoning the spirit of bacteriologist Dr. Shibasaburo Kitasato

(Editor's note: The CD of *Bussetsu Shoshinhogo*, the Japanese fundamental sutra of Happy Science, is playing in the background.)

RYUHO OKAWA

Dr. Shibasaburo Kitasato, the founder of the Kitasato University Hospital.

Dr. Shibasaburo Kitasato, doctor of bacteriology.

Dr. Shibasaburo Kitasato,

Who came up with ways to fight against the plague.

Please come down and teach us the critical or main points on how to deal with the coronavirus that is going around. How much do you know about this?

Dr. Shibasaburo Kitasato. Please come down here.

Dr. Shibasaburo Kitasato.

[*About five seconds of silence.*]

KITASATO

This is Kitasato.

A

Hello. Nice to meet you.

KITASATO

I heard I'll be on the (¥1,000) bill.

A

Yes.

KITASATO

Let's hope the Bank of Japan lasts until then.

A

Thank you for this opportunity today. Now, the novel coronavirus seems to be covering the entire world. How do you see this situation?

KITASATO

People use the word *pandemic*, but nobody knows the truth. Everyone thinks they will be able to enjoy the Olympics and see cherry blossoms next year. People think they will return to their everyday lives soon, after spring break. Most Japanese people think like that, but now, the number of infected people is increasing rapidly around the world. The infection is spreading rapidly in the bigger cities, but will also spread in poor countries from now on.

A

Now, the U.S. and... Oh, Africa.

China's cover-up is delaying the development of a vaccine

KITASATO

If China cultivated the virus in the lab, they have to come clean about it. That's the way to come up with a countermeasure... China must work with researchers in advanced countries to quickly make a vaccine, but they hide the truth by saying the U.S. attacked, which is making the situation more confusing. This is causing a delay in the development of a vaccine. If people could get information on what China was doing at the beginning of their research, they might be able to make the vaccine in a shorter amount of time.

A

I see. Since we must start by analyzing the virus itself...

KITASATO

Right. How they cultivated it.

A

That's right.

KITASATO

Actually, the person who made this virus can make a vaccine quickly. But now, China is trying to conceal it. The people whose existence could prove this likely disappeared as a means of destroying evidence.

A

Hmm, I see.

KITASATO

In Wuhan, even people who made this virus disappeared. I think so. China tries not to leave any evidence. They are deceiving the world into believing that the virus spread naturally, so in that sense, there will be a delay in dealing with it. Usually, when you invent weapons, you also develop countermeasures just in case. This is not a natural-born virus, apparently.

They should have had countermeasures. Maybe they thought about coming up with them but did not implement them because the people in charge would be executed. It's what you call a purge. This will seriously delay finding measures. Infections will spread widely, considering China is accusing the U.S. of this virus. So, the virus will spread because there will be a delay in finding ways to deal with it.

Also, Japan will not blame China because it wants to hold the Olympics next year, and will be slow in dealing with China.

China is definitely more polluted considering its poor sanitation

KITASATO

Inland China is definitely more polluted since its sanitary conditions are much worse than they are in Japan. Some parts of their main cities were improved to make them look better for foreigners coming in for the (Beijing) Olympics or the Shanghai Expo, but in other areas, their sanitary conditions are extremely poor. Speaking of sanitation, India and Africa are poor, too. Considering the high rate of infection in Europe and the U.S., hospitals of semi-developed and developing countries will be completely useless. Even if people are hospitalized, there are no vaccines, no treatments, and no hope to be saved.

So, in Japan, factories are asked to make oxygen inhalers (ventilators). They can make those. Oxygen inhalers can help patients suffering from pneumonia to breathe, but won't cure them. People try to keep them alive by helping them to breathe since they have trouble breathing, but there aren't enough beds available. Although many patients with oxygen inhalers are hospitalized, there is nothing hospitals can do.

China may be spreading a very deadly virus

KITASATO
After Chinese doctors arrived in Italy, many people died.

A
Yes, they did.

KITASATO
More than 10,000 people have died already (as of this recording). It's indeed strange. There may be some other reasons behind it. You need to do further research on this.

I find it strange for the mortality rate to keep changing. At first, it was very low. Now, it's gradually increasing. I believe the virus was designed to kill massive amounts of people. If it was made for mass murder, the outcome will be quite devastating.

A

The mortality rate was low at first, but...

KITASATO

It's getting higher.

A

What could be the reason?

KITASATO

Hmm, they could still be spreading it.

A

You mean, still spreading the virus, not the other way around?

KITASATO

Yes.

A

No way!

KITASATO

They could still be spreading it. They could have been researching something that can make the virus very potent to increase the mortality rate, even though they didn't have a way to wipe it out. In short, if they release cultured viruses in higher concentrations, it will get worse.

A

Oh, I see. I read an article in a Japanese magazine, either *Monthly Hanada* or *WiLL*, that said, "When the virus was first found in Wuhan, the Chinese government did not send medical units. They sent a major general of the army, the one in charge of biological weapons" and "This proved that China knew some of their own biological weapons were leaked."

KITASATO

They knew it from the beginning. In the beginning, they were humble. They even apologized. They thought it was their fault. However, once they noticed they would be sued for damages or punished, they made things more confusing instead. This country, which starts with the letter "C," always tries to destroy evidence. This is a huge problem because it prevents other countries from researching it.

Did China extract and culture a virus from bats in a cave?

KITASATO

I think Japan will suffer less than others. But although people are saying they will postpone the Olympics to July of next year (2021), I don't see how it'll be possible next year, either. The coronavirus pandemic is such a huge problem. It's not a problem that will be solved if only Japan could recover. Also, I don't think a vaccine will be ready next year.

A

You mean, it's a complicated virus?

KITASATO

It is a man-made virus. It's been made as a weapon...

A

Highly likely?

KITASATO

Yes, highly likely. China might have researched ways to make it more deadly. It's not a natural one. They might have extracted and mixed several things. Maybe they cultured viruses from different things. Bats are the most likely specimen. There is a very high possibility that China extracted viruses from bats in a cave somewhere in China. Not only that, but they must have cultured the particularly malignant ones in higher concentrations. During this process, it was leaked (outside). Probably.

A

Yesterday, I was researching about the plague and found some really frightening numbers. The mortality rate was 60 to 90 percent...

KITASATO

Right. And, it (the mortality of the novel coronavirus) is already over 10 percent in Italy.

A

It seems the world population was reduced by one-fourth back then.

KITASATO

In Japan and China, at the beginning of all this, the mortality rate of the virus was considered as low as the common cold...

A

Yes, it was like that.

KITASATO

People believed it would not be as high as the flu, but it is getting higher. So, there's something wrong.

A

I see.

"An army of Grim Reapers are going to every single hospital"

A

How is the Spirit World reacting to this?

KITASATO

Well... It seems like many Grim Reapers are being summoned. A huge number of people, more than usual, are expected to return to the other world. So, it's as if an army of Grim Reapers are going to every hospital.

A

You mean, the coronavirus was first recognized as something like a cold or the flu, but it might get worse.

KITASATO

In the past, the world overlooked China. There were MERS and SARS, originally from China, and even in those times, the viruses that China had been studying leaked out.

A

I see.

KITASATO

They leaked. But no one bashed China, right?

A

Right. People didn't investigate China.

KITASATO

Once the virus outbreaks settled down, that was the end. But they must have been studying deadlier ones.

Did China launch a virus attack because they cannot beat the U.S. in a nuclear war?

A

Americans are filing lawsuits against China.

KITASATO

China has no hope of winning in a nuclear war against the U.S. So, they tried another way, a virus attack. They were thinking of attacking with electronic weapons, but if the U.S. gets serious, they probably can't win. If it's a virus-type attack, no one will know who the culprit is. If China says the situation is under control now...

A

That's questionable.

KITASATO

The one China leaked first could've been less deadly, and...

A

Ah, they leaked it within China…

KITASATO

They might have brought a stronger (more deadly) one abroad. Now, China is trying to prevent people from coming from abroad. China could be trying to make it look as if they're not the culprit.

A

Oh! I see. They calculated that far.

KITASATO

China doesn't care even if their people die. They think nothing of 3,000 deaths. It's definitely questionable that they don't have any newly infected people. If their statistics are true, they must have brought one with a higher mortality rate to other countries after they found that the one with a lower mortality rate leaked in December…

A

Yes, there is something odd going on in Italy. The virus widely spread after they accepted Chinese doctors.

KITASATO

It also went to Spain. After that, the coronavirus spread to destroy the entire EU. China could go to those nations to rescue and take them over. They could use such a strategy.

You can't say that the modern Genghis Khan[*] won't take over countries using this virus. China could have done a good amount of research and could have a good understanding of the characteristics of the virus. It's only spreading a lot and killing many people in countries other than China. This is possible if there is a huge gap in research levels. They may have thought about taking revenge on the U.S. when economic sanctions were imposed. I don't know whether the infection in China was an accident or occurred on purpose, but looking at their swift shutdown of Wuhan, they might have done it knowing how to control it to some extent. If so, this is a war using a biological weapon.

---

[*] According to spiritual readings conducted by Happy Science in the past, the first emperor of the Mongol Empire, Genghis Khan, is likely reborn as Xi Jinping. See *China's Hidden Agenda: The Mastermind Behind the Anti-American and Anti-Japanese Protests* (New York: IRH Press, 2012).

2

China's Virus War—
Its Aim and Expected Damage

Kitasato predicts, "In the end, at least 500 million people in the world will die"

KITASATO

It may... My prediction is not accurate enough at this point, but... What's the date? March 29 or 30?

A

It's the 30th.

KITASATO

Now, there are over 700,000 infected people (in the world) as of the 30th and I think many are still untested. The virus is spreading quite fast, so in the end, I think at least 500 million will die.

A

In the world?

KITASATO

In the world, 500 million people will die. I'm afraid to mention the number in Japan. Even if Happy Science's efforts reduce the spreading, at least 50,000 will die.

A

That's a huge number.

KITASATO

So, I can't predict what kind of economic and business activities people will be able to do in such a situation.

Is China trying to destroy Christian countries?

KITASATO

I'm very concerned that Catholic countries, especially Italy, where the Vatican is located, have been under attack. It seems that destroying Christianity is one of the missions that they have.

A

Ah, I see. There are many Christian groups in Europe.

KITASATO

Yes. It seems China is trying to destroy Christian countries, both Catholic and Protestant.

A

Do you know why there are more and more infected people in the U.S.?

KITASATO

Yes, yes. China may have brought in the virus. How would people be able to notice this? If the virus was brought in during the early stages, nobody would probably notice it. Security was not so strict at that time. If they brought the virus into the U.S. in January, it would have been impossible for anyone to notice it. All they needed to do was to set a trap and run away. No one would know.

People should realize that the situation is worse than they think. Japanese hospitals will come to an end soon, or in other words, the time will come when people will get infected by going to hospitals.

A

But the entire world must act to investigate the cause of this infection, right?

KITASATO

Right. Japan, especially, should be doing the most.

A

(Japan is) No-good.

KITASATO

Japan tries to protect China. Happy Science claims that the virus originated in China and the U.S. argues the same, but the majority of Japanese people do not think that way. They pity China.

A

They do.

KITASATO

The president of the University of Tokyo appointed a student from Wuhan, China as a valedictorian and let her make a speech at the graduation ceremony. He treated her like a victim of the Great East Japan Earthquake.

A

Right.

"This is most likely a virus war"

KITASATO

I think China's plotting something. How can I say, the first victim... It's like in a mystery novel in which the person who appears to be the first victim is the criminal.

A

Yes, yes, yes. That's typical.

KITASATO

Right? The person whom people least suspect is actually the criminal. It is typical for the person who gets injured first or appears to be targeted by someone to be the criminal. This problem is most likely such a case. It is obviously quite strange for the mortality rate to rise after some time. Something is definitely wrong if the epicenter is less deadly than the other areas.

A

Something is surely wrong.

KITASATO

It can't be true that the mortality rate is higher in the remote areas. Some people say the virus spread because of kissing and shaking hands, but they already know that the virus is spreading to some extent.

A

Exactly. There is something wrong if the mortality rate is going up.

KITASATO

Right. This is...

A

This is not about hugs and such, is it?

KITASATO

No, I don't think so. People already knew. If people were saying those things without knowing the real situation, it would be understandable. But they were already talking about washing their hands and other measures. So, this is not just a matter of blowing your nose with a handkerchief or something like that.

So, first, China might be thinking about taking over Islamic countries too, but they don't need to fully destroy those countries for some time because they are oil producers. Also, China is in a superior position. But most Christian countries are superior to China.

So, this is most likely a virus war.

A

I see.

KITASATO

There is little you can do if this is the case. No matter how hard people try, a perfect vaccine... It's difficult to research a vaccine in this situation. Medical workers are overwhelmed with patients, so they have no time to research it, either. Something is obviously wrong.

If the developed nations weaken, China will necessarily be the world leader

A

Japanese people's view of China has not changed even though the virus spread from there. This delayed countermeasures and things went into a vicious cycle. And nobody has noticed it.

KITASATO

Japan was trying to invite Xi Jinping as a state guest. He intended to visit Japan as a state guest during the cherry blossoms season, right? But at that time, China needed to throw a punch at the U.S. because the two were engaged in an economic war.

A

Although the U.S. is accusing China, it just seems like Japan is working to guarantee Xi Jinping his position.

KITASATO

It doesn't make sense.

A

I agree. It doesn't make sense from the viewpoint of the Japan-U.S. alliance.

KITASATO

China is probably trying to break up (the Japan-U.S. alliance). The fatality rate is a little lower in Japan. It's highly likely that a virus different from the one that spread in China also spread in other nations. You don't need such a large number of people to spread it. If a nation commits a crime like what Aum Shinrikyo did*, it will be a nightmare.

---

* Aum Shinrikyo committed a series of crimes, the most notorious being the Tokyo subway sarin attack on March 20, 1995. Members of the group released sarin gas on three Tokyo subway lines, killing 13 people and injuring 6,300.

A

I see. That's true.

KITASATO

Hmm... In short, developed countries consume. China is trying to reduce its military power and consumption.

A

I see. If the developed nations weaken, China will necessarily be...

KITASATO

The world leader.

A

And China can take advantage of developing countries.

KITASATO

Yes, right. But I don't think vaccines will be developed in just three years or so.

A

The world should investigate to find the true cause of the virus outbreak in Wuhan, China.

KITASATO

China is a closed nation, despite being so large.

The resulting damage could be as bad as the Black Death or the Spanish flu

KITASATO

As far as I can see, the virus was man-made and used as a biological weapon. Eventually, the mortality rate will... it will get much higher. You won't be able to escape. You can't.

If people can't see each other... No nations, other than totalitarian ones, are able to close themselves off completely. Only totalitarian nations can do this. North Korea may be able to shut themselves out. The point is, this kind of virus is the most dangerous for democratic nations because it keeps them from conducting democratic politics. Hmm. You must be more suspicious of this case. I don't think a natural virus can cause something like this. You should expect damage as bad as the Black Death or the Spanish flu.

A

It is really serious.

KITASATO

I don't know how far it will eventually go, but people are still thinking too optimistically.

A

People somehow think that this infection is much milder than the Black Death or the Spanish flu.

KITASATO

People think it can be prevented by wearing masks and washing hands. But if it is a weapon, it will be much worse. We are facing such a serious situation. People should know that more than 100 million people might die.

Most people don't think such a serious thing is happening now. They still think they can prevent the pandemic somehow. Even after seeing more than 10,000 coffins in Italy, they still think it occurred by chance.

A

Some reports say that about 80 percent of infected people have recovered so far.

KITASATO

There will be a second and third wave of infections.

A

I see. Is it better to ask Mr. R. A. Goal about it, too?

KITASATO

I don't know him. Anyway, I see this as a very serious case.

This is a "murder virus" that is trying to destroy democracy by encouraging an AI society

KITASATO

We don't have any countermeasures now but to keep people isolated. The only option is to put people in solitary confinement and keep them from interacting with each other. But if you do that, economic activities will stop.

A

We also need to feed ourselves.

KITASATO

So, the second wave will cause another Great Depression. It will happen.

A

Yes, it will.

KITASATO

The world could enter an era in which AI (artificial intelligence) controls both politics and the economy.

A

That is what China is aiming for.

KITASATO

Yes, that is exactly it.

A

I see.

KITASATO

Everything will be judged and controlled by AI, not by human beings. This is a murder virus that is trying to destroy democracy. Japanese people are way too optimistic.

A

Right.

China aims to make democracy perish through mysterious illness and great economic defeat

KITASATO

How will this problem be solved in the end...

[*About 10 seconds of silence.*] China claims that the epidemic in Wuhan has been contained and there are no infected people. If this were true, it would mean they have something to stop the infection.

A

It would mean they have an anti-virus vaccine.

KITASATO

That would be the only reason.

A

Right.

KITASATO

There would be no other reason. How can there not be a single additional person infected in China?

A

It can't be true.

KITASATO

China is most likely lying. If they are saying they have reduced the number of infections, they must have been conducting some research on a vaccine. Even if that is the case, they won't reveal it to others.

China might negotiate with countries, saying they will help only the pro-Chinese countries that suffered a lot of damage. Something like the end of the world will come again. China wants people to die from a mysterious illness like this, suffer great economic defeat, and it wants democracy to perish. China hates things like the protests in Hong Kong, right?

A

Right.

KITASATO

So, they are trying to make it hard for the people there.

A

It was going in the opposite way in the beginning.

KITASATO

If protesters demonstrate like before during a pandemic, they will die. So, China made it hard for people in Hong Kong to go outside.

A

Do you mean that China intentionally took advantage of this situation instead?

KITASATO

Yes, yes, yes.

A

In fact, the virus leaked, but they could have taken advantage of this situation instead.

KITASATO

It's difficult to tell whether the virus leaked accidentally or on purpose.

A

Maybe it was not leaked on purpose, according to someone from outer space.

KITASATO

You need to ask him about that. But there will come an apocalyptic age. As Happy Science says, Japan is now trying to develop antibody immunity against the virus through faith in El Cantare. This is a test to see if it can reduce the virus.

A

There are many people who ridicule it. It is up to Japanese people to choose.

KITASATO

Yes, if the world savior is on earth. Or, people can fight against the plague as I did, but I think the current situation is much worse. It seems like China wants to destroy democracy.

3

The Truth of the Spirit World and Economic Outlook According to Kitasato

"I don't know whether it's the god of darkness or the legitimate God who will destroy humankind"

A

Are you conducting research on bacteria in heaven too, Dr. Kitasato?

KITASATO

Research on bacteria in heaven... Hmm... I'm not too comfortable with being asked like that. I'm at a loss for an answer.

A

What kind of world do you live in now?

KITASATO

Hmm. A world in which many researchers live.

A

A world of medical workers?

KITASATO

I'm keeping an eye on this issue. Bacteria are used in various ways. I know that. There are still truths in the Spirit World that humankind hasn't discovered, such as how bacteria and viruses are used. Modern medicine is yet to discover the true cause of influenza and AIDS.

Another thing is... Nations with many LGBT people are Christian. The coronavirus is spreading in these countries now. From the point of view of Christian countries, this might seem like divine punishment similar to what happened to Sodom and Gomorrah.

A

But China is not God. If China is behind this infection, it can't be divine punishment.

KITASATO

But I don't know whether it's the god of darkness or the legitimate God who will destroy humankind.

A

Ah. China is doing this partly with the power of (the god of) darkness.

KITASATO

Yes, yes, yes. I remember Confucius or someone giving a fearful prophecy: "All of China would go to heaven or hell. All 1.4 billion people will go to heaven or hell."[*]

A

Yes, right. They won't be judged as individuals, but as China as a whole, in determining whether they go to heaven or hell.

KITASATO

It seems to me that they are trying to create another kind of Spirit World. This is as far as my recognition goes.

---

[*] See Ryuho Okawa, *Koushi-Kairiki-Ranshin-o-Kataru* (literally, "Confucius Talks about Supernatural Things") (Tokyo: IRH Press, 2014), available only in Japanese.

If all economic activities stop,
Japan could return to the primitive age

KITASATO

If I dare say something to Japanese people now... [*Sighs.*] What can I say? It's a tough time. You might end up returning to the primitive age if worse comes to worst.

A

Oh, no!

KITASATO

If all economic activities stop, I mean.

A

That's true...

KITASATO

Right. You won't be able to trade or go abroad.

A

In that case, people who live in the countryside will be better off. They have more to feed themselves.

KITASATO

Yes, people might return to a primitive lifestyle. If the infection spreads explosively to India and Africa, it'll be the end.

A

Ah, yes. India is a rival of China, too, in a way.

KITASATO

Yes. I believe China also wants to do something against India. So, you shouldn't think optimistically. I can do another interview if you want to know more in detail, but there's a limit to how much I know. What I can say is that, for now, you should be quite afraid.

A

I see. I understand.

KITASATO

I should tell Japanese people, "About 50,000." Any more than this, I cannot say...

A

Oh? Could more than 50,000 possibly die in Japan?

KITASATO

If 50,000 people will die, that means more than a million people will be infected, right?

A

Oh, I see.

KITASATO

I don't know if the infection will stop at that level. I don't know whether Japan can survive if it shuts off the roads here and there and declares "martial law." But China might be thinking of ruling the world with biological weapons.

A

I understand.

Kitasato is one of the bodhisattvas of the healing spirit group

KITASATO

My opinion is not enough, but there are other specialists. So, you can ask them if you need to.

A

What kind of world do you live in?

KITASATO

There is the healing spirit group. I am like one of the bodhisattvas in it. There are other high spirits, including Pasteur and Koch.

A

I understand. Thank you very much.

KITASATO

OK.

RYUHO OKAWA

[*Claps twice.*]

CHAPTER TWO

Analysis of the Future from Space

-Spiritual Messages from R. A. Goal-

Originally recorded in Japanese on March 30, 2020,
in the Special Lecture Hall of Happy Science in Japan,
and later translated into English.

R. A. Goal

A space being from Planet Andalucia Beta in Ursa Minor. One of the commanders of the space defense force. A certified messiah.

1

"Virus War" Started by China

China may have abandoned treatment

(Editor's Note: The CD of *Bussetsu Shoshinhogo*, the Japanese fundamental sutra of Happy Science, is playing in the background.)

R. A. GOAL

Yes. I'm R. A. Goal.

A

Thank you for your continued support. We are sorry to have asked you to come again today.

R. A. GOAL

Not at all. I thought you might call me.

A

Earlier, we asked Dr. Kitasato Shibasaburo about the coronavirus from the perspective of a medical doctor rather than from a terrestrial perspective. Do you see anything that has changed compared with when it all started?

R. A. GOAL

Hmm... [*about five seconds of silence*]. Yes. The numbers in China are being outpaced by the increasing number of infections in other countries. This is a question to be raised. It's unnatural. It looks as if China has conquered the virus.

A

We actually don't have a vaccine for it either.

R. A. GOAL

It's strange.

A

Yes, no matter how you look at it, it's strange.

R. A. GOAL

It's strange, but it's because the country can manipulate the information. Regardless, let us analyze the future by using our space level scientific technology.

Hmm… [*about 10 seconds of silence*]. Hmm… [*about 10 seconds of silence*]. We see that on a global level, there is a war of willpower such as between nations, between races, or between religions vs. anti-religions.

Hmm. The U.S. seems to be prepared for death tolls of several hundred thousand people out of millions of infected people. But if China, the country that started this virus, escapes responsibility for the outbreak of viral infections just by saying, "It's settled" the U.S. will not forgive China. It's not right.

A

Yes, indeed. It is likely that a war of words will be fought between the U.S. and China over the coronavirus.

R. A. GOAL

China may possibly have already abandoned treatment by medical workers.

In China, thousands of people have died. So, it is possible that medical workers have already abandoned their duties, making it impossible to calculate the exact number. They are somehow trying to bounce back, but the point is to what extent they can control information. If the information is leaked, uprisings will be sure to occur in the country. So they are in a difficult situation. If they say that the pandemic has completely subsided, protests against the government will start. So they are waiting to see how things go. If protest movements or demonstrations start, they need to issue a curfew. I have a feeling that they wait and see how things will go and manipulate the figures.

When the U.S. and other countries regain energy to spare, they will investigate China

A

To find out the cause of the coronavirus, we need to keep our eyes wide open and question China.

R. A. GOAL

At present, other countries are busy worrying about their own patients. This is where we stand now.

But the U.S. has started to file a class action suit against China. So, when they regain some energy to spare, it will increasingly gain steam.

A

That's the American way of thinking.

R. A. GOAL

Japanese people are not good at this.

A

They never think of it.

R. A. GOAL

For example, they would never dream of demanding compensation for getting a cold from others. They would never think of demanding compensation for getting the flu from others.

A

No.

R. A. GOAL

They can't file a lawsuit, claiming, "That person has passed the flu on to me!"

A

The Japanese may feel sorry for everyone who caught the flu.

R. A. GOAL

It's possible in the U.S. They can do it. On the other hand, China can strike back at the U.S., saying, "No. We didn't."

A

Yes, I guess China will say so.

If it were a virus weapon, it could be spread by drone

R. A. GOAL

Considering the population density, my prediction is... the infection of the coronavirus is not so widely spread in Taiwan and Hong Kong. I think it's remarkable. They shut it out from China completely. It's amazing. Hmm. [*About five seconds of silence.*] Well, Mr. Trump is scheduled to run for the president. So, it is unlikely that he will just back off until Fall, while the country keeps suffering huge damage and a great depression, or an economic crash.

A

Is the virus spreading in New York City because so many people went back and forth?

R. A. GOAL

[*About 20 seconds of silence.*] Well, if this were a virus weapon, it could spread to some extent. It would be easy. At present, as (the guardian spirit of) Xi Jinping says, no one will know even if the virus is spread in the air using a drone.*

A

Master (Ryuho Okawa) has been concerned about drones because, in the spiritual message from the guardian spirit of Xi Jinping, he often kept saying, "You must have used drones."

R. A. GOAL

Yes, yes, yes.

A

The reason why he talked about drones so often is because...

R. A. GOAL

(They are) thinking about the use of drones.

---

* The author recorded "Spiritual Interview with the Guardian Spirit of Xi Jinping" on February 26, 2020. This session is available for view at all Happy Science temples and branches worldwide.

A

Master said that China itself could be planning on such aerial spraying of the virus. I thought, "That makes sense." The word "drone" was actually mentioned frequently.

R. A. GOAL

Drones can now deliver parcels just like a courier. So, if a drone drops a package full of viruses from above, it is certain to spread. Even if they drop the package in a densely populated district, almost no trace will be left behind.

China may have multiple viruses with different levels of lethality

A

According to Dr. Kitasato, "The fatality rate in Italy is increasing beyond the rate when the outbreak first occurred in China. That's a strange point." He said so. "If the virus is consistently the same, the fatality rate in China should have been as high as in Italy. It should have been. But as time passes, the fatality rate is increasing higher and higher." "The virus may have been leaked along the way and China just took advantage of that, and spread a slightly different virus around the world than the one in the initial outbreak."

R. A. GOAL

Yes, they could do that. Well, we can decontaminate it from above. But if we decontaminate the virus, humans may also be exterminated. So we need to be careful. If we decontaminate all creatures, humans will also die off.

A

Because humans and viruses are both living organisms.

R. A. GOAL

That's right. It is possible for us to decontaminate all the creatures.

But it is true that the longer this virus lingers, the more people will have antibodies. This can happen if it is the same virus. The antibody against the virus will be formed. If a certain amount of them are accumulated, then vaccines can be created. But the question (that Dr. Kitasato was mentioning) is what if China has several viruses. Yes, there is a possibility that virus No.1 is different from virus No. 2. If that is the case, the fatality rates will be different.

A

I see.

"Taking advantage" of the virus leakage?

A

I remember when you first taught us how we should see the coronavirus.[*] Is there anything that has changed in your view since then? Or is it OK that we stick to your initial view?

---

[*] Refer to *Spiritual Reading of Novel Coronavirus Infection Originated in China* (Tokyo: HS Press, 2020)

R. A. GOAL

This is a war of intelligence. It's a really tough battle.

A

A counterpart or an opponent exists at the other end.

R. A. GOAL

Yes, this is a war of intelligence and that makes it tough. There is a possibility that they are attacking Christian countries and developed countries using the virus. At the same time, the economic destruction of China continues. China's plan to conquer the world economy is now collapsing.

A

That means in the face of this crisis, the ability of each country is being tested, right?

R. A. GOAL

Yes, it is. So, hmm... since China suffered such a severe "tariffs attack" from the U.S., and they were demanded to reduce their trade surplus, it is no wonder that China had an urge to deliver a blow to the U.S. But if they used missiles, they must pay the price more.

The U.S. has its Seventh Fleet. So if they wanted a way to attack that would not be detected by the Seventh Fleet, then a virus weapon is of course an option. This type of weapon can't be identified.

A

But if that is the case, it means that China didn't deliberately leak the virus at first, but later on, decided to take advantage of the accident to use in their favor?

R. A. GOAL

So, the fatality rate of virus No.1 was less than five percent. A less vicious virus. After China leaked it, it would take some time until it spread around the world. So, they may have set up other viruses in other places. This is conceivable as a counterattack. It's possible. Even North Korea would do that if they were cornered militarily.

A

Use a biological weapon?

R. A. GOAL

They have missiles and biological weapons. It has been thought that North Korea may very well use those weapons first. If they attack Japan, it won't necessarily be with a nuclear weapon. If they use a nuclear weapon, it will easily and clearly draw retaliation. But in the case of a biological weapon, no one will actually know if it is even used. If a biological weapon is used as an attack, and North Korea sent junk fishing boats to the waters off the coast in the Sea of Japan, and they operated drones from there and had the drones drop a biological weapon, there would be little chance of knowing what happened. If a biological weapon is dropped at night, no radar can detect it, and no evidence is left behind. This type of attack was expected.

The ultimate goal of China

R. A. GOAL

I'm not sure whether or not this will be revealed to the public. Although it is almost certain that the virus originated in a research institution in Wuhan, it is hard to say to what extent the leakage was deliberate. But we knew the information in January. But in reality, no one knows if it will cause a pandemic unless it is actually done. They, too, were not sure how far the virus would spread. So, I believe they may have wanted to test it and see what would happen.

A

In China?

R. A. GOAL

Yes. Using a less deadly virus at first. They wanted to see how far the virus would spread. So, perhaps, initially, they may have just calculated that the tens of thousands of people in Wuhan would die to the least.

Because there are 11 million people there (Wuhan's population), it doesn't matter to China if thousands or even tens of thousands of people die. That's one possibility.

A

Did they develop the virus under the assumption of that level of death tolls and did they have that type of virus initially?

R. A. GOAL

Yes, that's right. In the beginning, there were not so many deaths. They considered its toxicity to be weak. In Japan, the incidence rate is still low. So it is likely that they may have been trying not to spread the virus in Japan out of consideration for Xi Jinping's visit to Japan. In any case, their ultimate goal is to divide the tie between Japan and the U.S., and perhaps the tie between the U.S., UK, and EU. Then, China will offer help to the EU. They were probably designing such a scenario. However, things may not go the way they want because something might arise. The cause of the virus is now being studied across the world. Eighty percent of the countries in the world other than Japan has already almost certainly concluded that the virus originating in China is not a naturally derived virus.

A

We need to detect the cause of the virus to produce vaccines for antibodies.

R. A. GOAL

That's impossible.

A

Without finding out the nature of the virus, it can't be done.

R. A. GOAL

That's correct. The world has already started to develop them, though. If China is several years ahead of other countries in its research, then they have more information. Undoubtedly, they have conducted various experiments about, for example, what concentration level of the virus kills people. There is no doubt that they study which viruses can kill people. If they have these research results, they must disclose them. However, after a virus originating in China has killed lots of people around the world, do you think China will voluntarily announce that they have something effective against it? It's unlikely for now. Therefore, unless countries other than China study it...

2

The U.S.'s Strategy for Dealing with China

If the U.S. concludes that the outbreak of the virus was an intentional attack by China, they may "attack Beijing"

R. A. GOAL

What can be assumed now is that if the U.S. or Mr. Trump concludes that, "The outbreak of the virus was an intentional attack by China against Western countries," then Mr. Trump may impose sanctions against China. It is likely that he will make such a decision. And if he finds evidence of an attack by a biological weapon, he will definitely do it.

A

Honestly speaking, Japan would never be able to do that. The only remaining scenario for justice to be established is for Mr. Trump to clearly state, "The virus came from China."

R. A. GOAL

That's why China is trying to hide it, while they (the U.S.) is trying as hard as they can to find it.

A

He (President Trump) has already mentioned it in various ways such as by calling it "the Chinese virus."

R. A. GOAL

At the moment, it appears that various people, including the CIA, are working to uncover the cause and evidence. Even in the case of Saddam Hussein, they attacked Iraq. And once the evidence is found, Mr. Trump will announce it, which should be before the presidential election. The U.S. is working hard to get evidence. Once they get the evidence, they may announce an attack on Wuhan or Beijing as sanctions by taking into consideration the degree to which the virus spread in New York.

A

Is there any possibility of that?

R. A. GOAL

Yes, there is.

A

Hmm.

Conspiracy theories about the U.S. to prevent China from getting attacked by the U.S.

R. A. GOAL

If the U.S. gets evidence of a biological attack against them, it would not be surprising if they launched ballistic missiles into China. But, if that happens, China may not be able to fight back. This is the reason why China is saying that the virus could be of U.S. origin or that it might have been set up by the U.S. Army. It appears that China is insisting on this to prevent such an attack.

A

If not, they normally wouldn't dare say something like that.

R. A. GOAL

Right? It's to prevent an attack by the U.S.

A

The moment when China said so, it made me realize, "Oh! China really did it."

R. A. GOAL

Now, what we see is that China might have had virus No.1, virus No.2, and virus No. 3. This is our current analysis. China aims to divide the Japan-U.S. alliance. Then, in regards to the EU, China is going to take possession of their banking, economy, and trade system through its "One Belt, One Road Initiative," which is China's way of providing salvation by incorporating others under its umbrella. Then, by isolating the U.K. and the U.S. from the world, by making Japan come under its rule, it plans to overpower Taiwan and Hong Kong. Even Taiwan would not resist it if it was struck by a virus weapon. Considering this, if Mr. Trump gets evidence, he will attack. If my thinking is the same as his, then I think he would not hesitate to launch intercontinental ballistic missiles into China before the presidential election. If there is a preliminary skirmish, the U.S. Seventh Fleet will launch conventional missiles into Wuhan and Beijing. Bombers will fly over from an island in the south... What was the name of that island? It's not Hawaii. It's a little more...

A

Is it Guam?

R. A. GOAL

Guam. Bombers would take four hours from Guam. They may fly and possibly attack from above. (Note: Currently, there are also reports that the bomber will be withdrawn to the mainland U.S. It is not possible to determine whether this is due to fear of a Chinese attack or is a diversionary tactic.)

If China did it knowing that its own country would be damaged as well, it was a clever trick

R. A. GOAL

Surprisingly, the U.S. was most wary of cyber-attacks. They had been most prepared for a cyber-attack. Not this type of virus but rather an electronic virus that would be used to halt the satellites and various U.S. Missile systems. They first expected those to be targeted. So they tried to defend themselves by putting pressure on Huawei. However, I think they are now suspecting that biological weapons were used instead. That's their judgment. So, what will the American president do? He will most likely announce it, and definitely attack Beijing and Wuhan as the first step. Next, they will probably decide whether or not to shoot each other with nuclear weapons. China probably won't want that.

A

I wonder why China didn't expect the U.S. to find out.

R. A. GOAL

They're planning it out now.

A

Right, I see. I understand.

R. A. GOAL

The virus emerged from their country and citizens from their country have died too, so their logic is that they can pretend to be the victim. That's true. If they did it knowingly, they are cunning.

A

But you're saying that there is a possibility that the timing wasn't exactly what China was planning.

R. A. GOAL

That's possible.

A

The timing when it all began.

R. A. GOAL

That is possible.

We already knew about this in January. But there were many seeds of war... A war in Iran was about to take place around January. Just around then, this (the outbreak of the novel coronavirus infection) happened. Well, that shows how North Korea, China, and Iran may be connected to some extent. Russia may be somewhat involved too. So, it is possible that there is a power struggle going on.

I had predicted already that the coronavirus would, in the end, spread to a certain extent.

A

You used the word astronomical from the beginning.

R. A. GOAL

Yes. I knew it.

The U.S.: A country with belief in God and judging "right or wrong"

R. A. GOAL

The U.S. is a nation that always strives for justice and would never forgive something that is wrong.

A

Mr. Stephen Bannon (the former White House Chief Strategist and senior adviser) wrote something very good: "What separates China from others is whether or not they possess the concept of God."

R. A. GOAL

"A materialist nation will not be forgiven."

A

Yes. "Because the Chinese Communist Party believes that God doesn't exist, do they not believe in the existence of heaven and hell, and do they not think about helping the Chinese citizens in their country and people in the world.

That is why they continue to lie, hide information, and spread crises throughout the world." That is what he said.

R. A. GOAL

(The Chinese Communist Party thinks) viruses and humans, aren't that different, right?

A

Yes, that's right.

R. A. GOAL

That's what they're like.

A

They cannot judge between values of good and evil from the eyes of God.

R. A. GOAL

No, atheist nations cannot. That is why Mr. Bannon declares that such atheistic nations should be crushed.

A

Yes. I thought Americans are really great.

R. A. GOAL

They are great. Their awareness is higher.

A

Even if someone in Japan said such a thing now, Japanese people would not respond.

R. A. GOAL

Well, Ryuho Okawa is the only one that would say such a thing.

A

Yes. That's right.

R. A. GOAL

Most wouldn't listen well, would they?

A

No. But the U.S. president, whose right hand used to be someone like that, is working now.

R. A. GOAL

Yes.

A strategy to end China's dogmatism is awaiting them

R. A. GOAL

Bunshun and Mr. Hiroshi wrote that Ryuho Okawa wants to be like the president of the U.S., but it's the opposite. Ryuho Okawa is guiding the president of the United States, both spiritually and in a worldly sense.

A

Right.

R. A. GOAL

In fact, El Cantare is currently guiding the president of the United States and leading him, so the next move is to reduce China's military power and lower China to the level of a moderately developed nation. This strategy has now begun to make China collapse economically, collapse militarily, and end the dictatorship. That's the scenario you're calling for. The U.S. is saying they will side with

Hong Kong and Taiwan, right? After this, this strategy will follow. So, the plan includes the fall of Beijing as well but Mr. Abe is thoughtless and is trying to have it both ways (with the U.S. and China), so Japan is being ignored.

A

Well, Japan is a little...

R. A. GOAL

Japan is being completely ignored.

A

Hmm. It's sad.

R. A. GOAL

The U.S. isn't including Japan in its plan. It's pointless to say anything to Japan.

A

In fact, it may only be a hindrance to the U.S.

R. A. GOAL

Yes, right. They're just saying, "Please stop."

A

That's right.

R. A. GOAL

Also North Korea... Oh, South Korea is completely abandoned by the U.S.

A

Hmm. I guess so.

R. A. GOAL

The U.S. thinks they are not worth existing anymore or that they cannot tell between right and wrong. A war might start next.

A

Well, either way, even without the virus, the world was on the verge of war.

R. A. GOAL

In fact, there is a virus panic now but after this, the countries that were invited to join the "One Belt, One Road Initiative" will eventually realize that they were being targeted for invasion. European countries in the financial crisis and African countries were on the verge of acquisition, and oil fields in the Middle East were almost taken. By eliminating the U.S., they were planning to take the oil fields. If they find out that China has provoked them with a virus attack, they (the U.S.) will not forgive them. They will attack fiercely. But the result will be good. People will die, but the world will move in a good direction.

A

Yes. Those who have clearly wrong values...

R. A. GOAL

Yes. So, it's like the Nazis are expanding, right?

A

Right.

R. A. GOAL

We must stop them from taking over the world. That is why Mr. Trump is now trying to be Winston Churchill. He's thinking he will lose if he is weak-minded so they are trying hard to discover a fault in them and they have a pretty good guess already.

The U.S., preparing for the struggle for supremacy of the Earth

A

Even a Japanese conservative magazine wrote that "a Chinese female researcher published a paper and gave a lecture on the development of the coronavirus."

R. A. GOAL
Right.

A

It was also written that "the reason why we found out about how there are people who research such things is that there was an insider's accusation by a female researcher who revealed that 'a research center in Wuhan, China is conducting an experiment to create an artificial virus' and the battle of the woman has begun."

R. A. GOAL

It's really only Japan that is living in a world that's so far from reality. They're still in the Meiji Period (1868 - 1912). Because they are saying that it would be good to have a sea of friendship and for everyone to live peacefully.

The next crisis to come after the coronavirus will be a war for hegemony over the Earth. The sooner it happens, the more favorable for America. The later it becomes, China will try to advance more favorably. Next, India will become involved. Mr. Trump went to India to maintain a good relationship between America and India, so I think they are thinking of dealing with China from both sides. After all, India has nuclear weapons too. So if worse comes to worst... We should not overlook the fact that Mr. Trump visited Mr. Modi at that time.

A

That's true.

R. A. GOAL

The infection had...

A

Already started at the time.

R. A. GOAL

Over 100,000 people gathered to welcome the president at the time the infection had started to spread. So, I think China's strategy is, more or less, seen through. The plan to disintegrate the Chinese Empire will, after this, begin as a counterattack.

Secret attack on China that the U.S. has in mind

R. A. GOAL

However, the method of retribution is unknown. America

may have a secret way to attack that no one knows about. There may be methods to attack that are quite surprising.

A

Right, after all, the U.S. is the most advanced.

R. A. GOAL

Yes. One of the special developments by the U.S. is a weapon that can artificially cause earthquakes. They have already developed this. With Chinese quality buildings, if an earthquake is artificially triggered, 100,000 to 200,000 people would immediately be killed. So they have an earthquake weapon already. That's one. The other is, they are thinking of an attack that would stop China from making an electromagnetic pulse. So I believe it is possible that the U.S. will destroy China's satellites and all of their electronic payment systems. They can use a weapon in the form that destroys all Chinese electronic equipment and paralyzes all the functions of their Internet and electronic payment networks. Then, they will easily end up in a situation with no assets. This may happen. They are now thinking of several types of attacks and, considering the way China started the crisis, they are also trying to give back to them by making it an unexpected one. They are very lenient toward North Korea, but the U.S. is thinking nothing of them because they are actually easy to stomp on and crush.

A

The real root is...

R. A. GOAL

China.

A

Unless China changes, the gangster-like countries will never cease to exist.

R. A. GOAL

Yes, yes. They're thugs. If China is a gangster, the others are thugs.

A

Right, North Korea would be [*smiles wryly*].

R. A. GOAL

So, it will collapse easily. If we crush China, they'll collapse too.

3

The Path Japan Should Take

What's happening now is a disguised World War III

R. A. GOAL

Now, you have been trying to isolate China and cast an encircling net, but America is also going to do the same, so the strategy is similar.

A

Right, so, this year our organization is going to do the opposite of what China is planning. We are going to connect Japan, the U.K., and the U.S.

R. A. GOAL

Well, there are things that even Mr. Kitasato doesn't know about. What he's thinking about is the virus, and how infected people can die. That's what he is capable of thinking of, but we are thinking about politics and diplomacy as well. I think you need to ally with the U.K., the U.S., India, Australia, and countries in the Asia region, such as the Philippines, Indonesia, and Malaysia. Also Canada. China, Canada (pro-Chinese nation), and the pro-Chinese nations of EU with Germany at the center are what you must defeat. EU nations operating through Chinese capital are something that must also be defeated. To state it bluntly, unlike how they were in the past, this is World War III in disguise. It may progress and end without anyone realizing that it was World War III. People may not know. The previous was also the Cold War. World War III actually ended without launching a missile.

A

There are times you can later find out through various movies or documents that it was virtually a state of a war in which classified information was actually flying around.

What's important is to continue saying that "China is the culprit"

R. A. GOAL

So, now, if it were possible for China to democratize itself, we could leave it to them, but we have determined that to be impossible. So, we will forcefully make it collapse. I think we are in agreement with what you're saying. Concrete attacks using military power and economic power will be launched, primarily by the U.S., but Japan will be satisfied with a diplomatic encircling network. However, Japan must not be sympathetic toward China as if it is a disaster-stricken area. They are the culprit. This year, it is important to continue saying this. Many people will die but the world will be purified. It's heading in a good direction. An atheistic country with a population of 1.4 billion people is trying to enlarge its nation, but we absolutely cannot allow this.

A

I truly feel that atheism and the tendency to mock things of the other world and spiritual messages still largely exist.

If this intensifies and goes so far as to ban religion, religion will be pushed underground.

R. A. GOAL

Yes. If you come under Chinese control, that's what will happen.

A

Yes.

R. A. GOAL

So, in a sense, it stopped Xi Jinping from landing in this country.

A

Right. In the film *Silence* (an American film released in 2016), Christians were being oppressed but I really feel that if China took over the nation and you were to live as a person of faith, that would be the only path left for you.

R. A. GOAL

You will have to die. So we stopped Xi Jinping from coming as a state guest.

A

Yes. It was prevented.

R. A. GOAL

Also, since the Emperor is young, Xi is taking him lightly. Mr. Abe, with his empty brain, thinks he is dealing with China on equal terms but Xi is aiming to contain and take over Japan. So we'd like to change (Japan's) national values and national policy to those of Prince Shotoku.*

A

Hmm! Prince Shotoku's values.

---

* Prince Shotoku (574 - 622) A member of the Imperial Family in ancient Japan. A politician. He accepted Buddhism, which was the most advanced religion at the time in the East, and built the foundation of the central government. He also pursued diplomacy with China on equal footing.

R. A. GOAL

Our plan is to change this Era into one in which the age of Prince Shotoku would happen today. We will not waste the 10 years of defeat of the Happiness Realization Party.

A

Wow...

R. A. GOAL

Yes. I plan not to. When values change, everything will be different. We will make "the pro-China virus" go extinct. Soon it will become exposed. It will become clear how China is the culprit. I think so.

A

Well, first of all, we need to discover the cause.

R. A. GOAL

Yes.

A

We really want them to find out.

R. A. GOAL

Happy Science cannot fight with weapons or directly move the economy, so basically you only have speech and action. That's why you need to say that the virus comes from China and it is an aggressive attack on the world by China. (On the other hand, China) is trying to acquire nations under the pretense of "helping them." I believe that they are actually trying to take over other nations by entering as if they have come to "help." Of course, if your medical technology is high, this can be pushed back. The other is that it is important for your values to oppose them.

"Atheist forces must be wiped out from Asia"

R. A. GOAL

Our aim is to liberate Tibet, Uyghur, Inner Mongolia, as well as Hong Kong and Taiwan. Nepal is being taken again by Mao Zedong factions, but this also needs to be liberated and atheist forces must be wiped out from Asia. We also plan to return Russia to being a democratic and liberal country. Russia must be made an ally, not an enemy. Australia must be brought in too. Japan should choose the direction that will make its economy stronger, not weaker. Japan is being Mr. Nice and scattering its money everywhere. They have hollowed out the industries in their own country and are helping other countries become strong. But we are trying to change that and create a situation in which they will have to redirect this towards increasing its national strength.

A

In any case, Japan needs to be more self-reliant...

R. A. GOAL

It's necessary.

A

Is that what you meant?

R. A. GOAL

That's right.

A

The Happiness Realization Party has been calling for self-reliance since its founding. Japan should be economically self-sufficient also.

R. A. GOAL

Yes. Energy too. Energy self-sufficiency is at a dangerous level.

A

On top of that, it's getting harder to use nuclear energy.

R. A. GOAL

Right?

A

Japan is increasingly more reliant on imports.

R. A. GOAL

Japan has no energy either. That's not good. Japan has to head toward becoming 100 percent self-reliant. You can't expect to get electricity from mainland China or the Gobi Desert. That's very bad. Not good at all.

A

We would be their hostage the second we did that.

R. A. GOAL

They would own you. To get electricity sent over through underwater cables? That's a very bad idea.

When looking ahead to 2050 from a macro level, now is clearly the time to act

R. A. GOAL

If you look at the period from now to 2050 from a macro level, you will see that now is the time to act. Give China more time and you will lose. You will surrender to the Chinese army. China plans to surpass the U.S. from 2025. The battle will begin before that. There will be all kinds of casualties. But the world will shift in the direction you speak of between 2020 and 2030. I do not know if you will be directly praised. Perhaps recognition is something that comes later. But you must do your utmost to spread Happy Science teachings across the world.

A

It's important that we continue.

R. A. GOAL

It's important. Do not let a virus deceive you. It's a part of their disruption strategy. They mean to disrupt the world. It is clear that they have their own plan, a global strategy. We must fight to retake the world. It is a difficult task. It is also a battle of intelligence.

4

China Aims to Block
the Re-Election of Mr. Trump

China is trying to turn Xi Jinping into "God"

R. A. GOAL

Right now, they are carefully making it seem like it is a naturally occurring virus. Next, they will insist it was an accident. Or, they will say that the U.S. attacked them. They will say that it is a virus weapon created by the U.S. military among many other things. But these are all things that China wants to do. That is one way to fight. But once Trump decides (to fight China), he will. If they fight now, the U.S. will win. It is still possible to beat China if you fight now. You can still win. But if there is a string of presidents like Barack Obama, then you cannot.

A

It will be a dark world.

R. A. GOAL

China will take over everything.

A

Yes, they will.

R. A. GOAL

Completely.

A

People like him cannot handle matters like this.

R. A. GOAL

They are very weak. Very weak.

A

If it is a life-threatening disease, the later the cause is identified, the more damage it will do.

R. A. GOAL

It's not easy. Trump may feel very strongly that he cannot let the presidency go to the Democrats. He knows he must win while he is President. China is out to spread the coronavirus in the U.S., make its economy plummet, cause a crash on Wall Street, lower the stock prices that Trump worked to raise, lower the economic growth rate and raise the unemployment rate in order to prevent him from getting re-elected.

A

I see.

R. A. GOAL

This is what China wishes to do most: to destroy Trump's chances of re-election. They definitely wish to do this. Especially at this time. They think if they do this much, Trump's popularity will go down. China has already turned Xi Jinping into God. When he visited Wuhan, the number of new coronavirus cases disappeared. That's the sort of country China is. They are making people worship him as God. I'm sure any Uyghur watching the coronavirus pandemic feels that they are being told, "This is how easy it will be to kill you." I'm sure that is how they feel right now. It's the same in Tibet. They probably feel like they are being shown what will happen if they revolt.

A

I understand.

R. A. GOAL

That's China's global strategy.

The reason why the novel coronavirus began to spread on December 8

R. A. GOAL

As to how many people will die, I cannot tell you yet. The word "astronomical" was mentioned, but the number of casualties will be large for sure. Also, there is a high possibility that a different kind of war may take place on top of this. It must happen before the U.S. presidential election. Otherwise, it wouldn't make sense. All in all, the first half of 2020 will be very tough.

A

What should ordinary people do? As you said in the beginning about the faith vaccine...

R. A. GOAL

You can fight with that. The fatality rate is still only about 10 percent. It may rise slightly, but the light cases should be no different from treating influenza. However, those whose physical condition has weakened will not make it. Killing off the old and the disabled is something the Nazis would think of doing, isn't it?

A

Right.

R. A. GOAL

China is struggling with the same problem. Their population is aging. So they want to kill them in the future. But it is wrong to think like that. Japan must also aim to create a society where the elderly can remain active and live full lives.

Well, it (coronavirus) is related to this domestic issue they (China) have. Domestically, it is enough to just kill the elderly and the disabled by a less deadly virus. But overseas, they want to think about killing healthy people as well as children and babies by a more deadly virus.

A

Xi Jinping's guardian spirit appeared agitated when the virus first got out. The virus is a part of his global strategy, but am I right to understand that the timing was not what he intended? Everything from the first spiritual message would line up if that was true.

R. A. GOAL

That's right. It happened on the same day Japan declared war on the U.S. It is also the Day of Conquering the Devils and Attaining Enlightenment.

A

December 8.

R. A. GOAL

December 8 was when it all began.

A

I see. December 8 is also the day John Lennon passed away. December 8 is...

R. A. GOAL

For some reason, the virus leaked on December 8.

A

I see. We shouldn't...

R. A. GOAL

I shouldn't say anything further.

A

Right.

R. A. GOAL

It's not possible to arrest us, though [*laughs*]. Just so you know.

Take the weapons away
from those who do not believe in God

A

Well, in every age, heaven expresses its intentions in different ways. There have been all kinds of people and all kinds of things have happened.

R. A. GOAL

I know. But even if it had been put off to a later date, China still planned to cause it before the U.S. Presidential Election.

A

I see. Because their aim is to stop Trump's re-election.

R. A. GOAL

If China had been given more time, it would have unleashed the virus on a much greater scale.

A

That was their plan.

R. A. GOAL

Now, did they deliberately leak the virus out into their own country knowing all this? Or did the virus get out by accident? That is hard to say. But one thing is true: They needed to test the virus to see if it would work or not.

A

Right.

R. A. GOAL

They needed to experiment in order to know if it would work in New York and in Europe. How else would you know? They want to test it somewhere, but people would raise eyebrows if they tested it on their autonomous regions. In the end, we could say that it may have happened by an accident. I would assume they had the intention to test it somewhere. Unfortunately, the world learned about the virus much sooner than they expected. Japan's health care system is advanced and sanitation conditions are quite good. Compared to the rest of the world, Japan's number of cases will remain low. I think so. Probably. But economically, there will be a recession. Japanese Prime

Minister Abe's economic policies will crumble. I'm sorry to say. The only thing that can be done about this is for the Happiness Realization Party to do its best.

A

It's still meaningful to voice our opinions, isn't it? At least it will get those who hear it to think about it.

R. A. GOAL

In any case, you need to create politics that believe in God. It is your mission.

A

Yes. When it comes to possessing weapons too, we don't want them in the hands of people who don't believe in God.

R. A. GOAL

No, no. They must be taken away from them. So, this is what I see happening.

5

The Time for the Battle that will Reveal "Humanity's Way Forward"

It's time for Japan to fulfill its national mission

R. A. GOAL

How the U.S. will retaliate will be quite interesting. I think they know almost everything. Japan, on the other hand, is only able to talk about the new number of infected people and ask people not to go out at night. Even when North Korea shot missiles over it, they could only sound the alarm and ask people to hide in shelters. Japan cannot remain like this.

A

It is in a way a brainwashed country. "Brainwashed country: Japan."

R. A. GOAL

Right. It must stop living in the post-war era.

A

Right.

R. A. GOAL

Stop living like it is still the post-war era. As for the mission of Japan, if the U.S. is going to take on the mission of dismantling China, I am sure Trump wants Japan to at least bring the Korean Peninsula under control. This is the least that is expected of Japan. It's not a lot to ask for. It is ridiculous that Japan can only plead for the abductees taken to North Korea to be returned. If that is all you can do, to the Americans, Japanese politicians are not political leaders.

The battle between the "God of Light" and the "God of Darkness" cannot afford to be lost

A

There have been wars between communism and liberalism in the past. World War II was largely caused by differences in political philosophies. What this means is that politics must have a philosophy, right?

R. A. GOAL

Mr. Trump is trying to become Winston Churchill, but you must become like Moses. You must go forth with a resolve so strong that you could split the Sea of Japan clean down the middle. Crush mistaken ways of thinking and rebuild Japan. This is the reason why the Happiness Realization Party was established. The mass media may laugh, but we will break them apart at the seams. This recession is necessary. Otherwise, we could not destroy them.

A

Hmm... I guess society's values wouldn't change if things remained the way they are now.

R. A. GOAL

Those who make their income from left-wing ideologies must no longer be able to do so. At any rate, many things will happen but Ryuho Okawa is a brilliant leader. He will show humanity the way forward. And the people of the world will come to believe it.

A

Xi Jinping wants to become God, but Master, the true God, is always humble, listening to the opinions and voices of the high spirits in heaven. He is completely different from Xi Jinping. It's a different style.

R. A. GOAL

It is Ahura Mazda battling Ahriman.

A

It really is.

R. A. GOAL

The God of Light battling the God of Darkness. Frankly, Xi is the God of Darkness. That is why he must be destroyed. We cannot afford to lose. If we do, then a lot of darkness in the universe will come in. We must never let it enter the Earth. We will not let that happen.

A

I see.

We will definitely liberate
Uyghur and Hong Kong by all means

R. A. GOAL

So, I believe the U.S. will make a move. But if they do not, or if what they do is not enough, then we will lend a hand. We will cause many mysterious things to happen.

A

I'm so sorry you would have to do that.

R. A. GOAL

This incident could be likened to, say, a nuclear missile exploding prematurely before China launched it. That's what it's like. China's secret plan got found out.

A

Which is why they were shaken too.

R. A. GOAL

Yes. They were planning to a few months later...

A

To launch it?

R. A. GOAL

Xi wanted to go to Japan first, be welcomed as a state guest, pull Japan firmly to its side, establish a strategically friendly alliance, and then cut the Japan-U.S. Security Treaty. That was his basic strategy.

A

I see.

R. A. GOAL

They wanted to make Japan feel it was better to side with China. In this way they wanted to control all of Asia, and then control Europe, then Africa. But we need to destroy this. Doing so will require a huge amount of power. But we will answer the pleas of "Please help Uyghur, please help Hong Kong," as it was said in Canada*. We will liberate them. To do so we need some level of strong-armed tactics. Many more things will happen soon. So, please stay strong.

A

Yes.

R. A. GOAL

It's important to learn Chinese, but I will work to make sure English becomes the dominant language.

A

I understand.

R. A. GOAL

Japanese too.

A

Right.

---

* In Toronto, Canada, an English lecture entitled, "The Reason We Are Here" and its Q&A session were held on October 6, 2019. On a later date, Master Ryuho Okawa answered questions and requests from participants from the lecture. They were Canadian liberation activists of Hong Kong and Uyghur (Refer to *The Reason We Are Here* [Tokyo: HS Press, 2020]).

R. A. GOAL

I want to make the Japanese language more prevalent in Asia, and I also want to make Japan have greater power so the nation will not disappear.

Now is the time to save people from anxiety and fear through passionate activity

R. A. GOAL

Regarding other matters, more voices from heaven will pour down through the voice of Ryuho Okawa. As a preliminary skirmish, the mass media will try to shake you up. And Ahriman's pawn, the devil, is using Mr. Hiroshi to cause problems, but this is precisely why you must do your job. You must not be defeated.

A

Yes.

R. A. GOAL

You must go above the politicians.

A

You're absolutely right.

R. A. GOAL

The one who determines the way of thinking of this country, this person (Master Okawa) is this country's supreme leader. But the one that is wasting the Diet's time by lying about the cherry blossom viewing party cannot make decisions. The decisions will be made here. We will spare no effort it helping you. We will protect you too if it comes down to it. Do not worry.

A

We on earth will do our best to spread this way of thinking God has given us.

R. A. GOAL

Japan's politicians will probably tell you to stay quiet and stop your activities, but I think, now is precisely when Happy Science must act passionately. Give out books passionately. Invite people to become members passionately. Be passionately active at the local branches and missionary centers and other locations you have. Those overseas should go about in their own way expanding further and further. You must not be scared.

A

I'm sure people outside are fearful and worried and their hearts are gloomy.

R. A. GOAL

Japanese people have been "tamed" by the values of the post-war, and this is the result of it. So you are approaching a time when the fundamental character of this nation will change dramatically.

A

Thank you so much for today.

R. A. GOAL

Yes.

PART TWO

Messages from R. A. Goal

Description when Part Two was recorded

Part Two consists of three messages given on March 17, 18, and 25, 2020, prior to the recording of messages from R. A. Goal in Part One given on March 30.

CHAPTER ONE

Warnings of
the Pro-China Mentality

-Spiritual Messages from R. A. Goal-

Originally recorded in Japanese on March 17, 2020,
in the Special Lecture Hall of Happy Science in Japan,
and later translated into English.

The situation when this chapter was recorded

This spiritual message session was recorded on March 17; it was after the WHO announced the "novel coronavirus pandemic" on March 12 and before the postponement of the Tokyo Olympics was finally decided on March 24.

1

Chinese-Style Development Will Be Fundamentally Lost

China is starting to adjust its number of novel coronavirus cases

RYUHO OKAWA

(*Calls the name with a tune.*) R. A. Goal, R. A. Goal, R. A. Goal, R. A. Goal...

(Editor's Note: The CD of *Bussetsu Shoshinhogo*, the Japanese fundamental sutra of Happy Science, is playing in the background.)

[*About 10 seconds of silence.*]

R. A. GOAL

I am R. A. Goal.

A

Thank you for your continued support.

R. A. GOAL

Yes.

A

Well, some materialistic media personnel are mocking Happy Science regarding the novel coronavirus.[*]

R. A. GOAL

It may be because they can't do anything, right?

A

Yes.

R. A. GOAL

Well, I guess different people can believe in different things.

A

Can you give us any inspirational words?

---

[*] At the time of the recording, a religious writer published an article that twisted the content of *Spiritual Reading of Novel Coronavirus Infection Originated in China* (Tokyo: HS Press, 2020) from a material perspective, and made unfounded defamation claims about Happy Science.

R. A. GOAL

Hmm... China is a country that always wants to put the blame on others [*laughs*].

A

[*Smiles wryly.*] It's unbelievable.

R. A. GOAL

China may blame religion if the coronavirus spreads when they have gatherings. Or they may say, "America is the one that started it all." They will say whatever they want to say. But what China actually fears are the withdrawal of investments made into its country and the interruptions they may face as they try to expand or do activities overseas. China has already started adjusting the number of coronavirus-infected people. They are reducing it intentionally. They deliberately ignore patients that exceed their doctors' capacity. So the number of infected people in China isn't increasing that much. In short, they announce manipulated numbers, saying that the outbreak of the coronavirus infection has passed its peak.

A

The guardian spirit of Xi Jinping said, "All we have to do to resurrect is to just announce that the number of infected people has passed its peak."

R. A. GOAL

Yes, they are reviving. They are starting to go out in crowds, open events again, and go on eating sprees.

A

They are even saying things like that the U.S. Army is the one that brought the virus into China...

R. A. GOAL

Because if the virus had been an attack by the U.S. Army, they could ignore it by pretending that it was over.

A

It is a terrible thing to say, though.

R. A. GOAL

Shall I tell you what the future holds as a result?

A

Yes.

R. A. GOAL

It means that it will spread more and more in Beijing.

A

You mean people in the city will get infected.

R. A. GOAL

Yes, the virus will surely infect more people in Beijing.

Future outlook on economic damage and of locust plague movement

R. A. GOAL

This is actually heaven's will. The will of heaven is trying to hold off what should not spread any further. It rejects the prevalence of the Chinese virus all over the world by closing the country. You had better know it. Furthermore, a great depression is about to spread throughout the world from China. You need to withstand these two. Another issue is a swarm of locusts from East Africa, with more than several hundred billion locusts flying over the desert. They are now going through Pakistan and are making their way toward China. They're arriving soon. China's wheat harvest is around May or June. They will probably come during the harvest season. At that time, China would say, "This is an 'insect weapon' from some other country" [*laughs*].

It is hard to explain the relationship between heaven's will and us, but the gods of the Earth are not just the people who were born on the Earth. We space people who have sent our offspring down to the Earth bear responsibility and we have been watching over the transitions of civilizations on the Earth for a long time. Such watchers, who intend to watch over this planet, are from places other than Earth. But they are beings who were recognized as gods in history. Things that are Chinese in origin are under the influence of bad space people. So, we are now creating a barrier to block these.

Well, the virus is now spreading to the U.S. and Europe. They are in panic mode and call it a pandemic. They created too many movies of that kind, so they are trembling with fear, like the movie where only one person survived in New York. I think they are afraid of such a situation. But what I predict is that their economy will suffer great damage. In the worst-case scenario, the economy will drop to 20 to 30 percent from its present scale. Although the world may face a recession, an opportunity to reconsider will appear.

So, Chinese-style development will be fundamentally lost. China may enter an age in which they will suffer food shortages, instead of making money in foreign countries.

Japan has a problem, too. Japan had a "Pro-China virus" or a "China-Welcome attitude" and allowed too many things from China to enter the country. But now the country is slowly starting to shut it out. This is a part of China's occupation policy, so Japan is now trying to weaken the influence of China and make changes. Japan needs to make its economy independent of China. Militarily speaking also, such a sense of independence will be necessary.

Globally, there are still many indications of wars in Africa or the Middle East, and in response to this, I believe it is necessary to have them feel heaven's warning again.

In Italy, too, they are suffering quite severely from the virus. It may be that the issue of Christianity or modern Christianity originating from the Vatican is coming to light. In South Korea, in most cases, wrong Christian religions are causing the issues related to the coronavirus. So that is why some people say that materialism is more advantageous. It's all materialistic to say, "wash your hands," "put on a mask," "gargle," or "avoid going places where people assemble." These are all based on materialism.

2

What the World Has to Realize Now

In times of an epidemic, it's natural that religions hold prayer services

A

Well, but it is strange for religion to do nothing as a means of saving people when plagues or other diseases become rampant.

R. A. GOAL

A religion prays, holds prayer services, and uses spiritual will power.

A

Yes, we pray, we hold prayer services. It's natural.

R. A. GOAL

Yes, it is a matter of course. It works.

A

People in Japan now don't seem to understand this, partly because they spend less time studying history.

R. A. GOAL

The reason why Mr. Hiroshi says—"What is wrong with using *Shoshinhogo* and a physical disability certificate for *Menko**** is that he does not have any idea of what "punishment by God" is. I hope people who know about the religions of the world—no matter how little—will know about divine punishment. As it occurred in the Exodus written in the Old Testament, those things happen in various religions.

Hmm, so, it is time for purification, and it is time to change one's mind. It is time that we need a Savior. You should do your activities fearlessly and with conviction. In Japan, Happy Science is working hard, so I expect that the coronavirus will not spread so widely. But I believe that the current administration should receive a certain divine punishment.

---

* A children's game of slapping cards on the ground to flip those of their opponents.

A

No one, including the mass media, knows anything yet...

R. A. GOAL

Yes. It's bad. It's not good at all. They ignored the Happiness Realization Party and insisted that religion is evil. Now, they feel a sense of helplessness over what the mass media, education, and politics should be, but this is a calculated result. If we only need to wash our hands and gargle... The way I see it, the precautions needed for the coronavirus infection are the same as those for the flu. It would not go beyond that (at the time of recording).

But, the Tokyo Olympic Games are just around the corner. If the Olympic games are held without any spectators [*laughs*], it will be unprecedented and will leave a stain on history. Whether it is held or not, it will either ways.* Now is the time for the world to become aware of something.

---

* On March 24, 2020, one week after this spiritual message was recorded, International Olympic Committee decided to postpone the Tokyo Olympics and Paralympics due to the spread of the novel coronavirus.

A

I wonder if they will.

R. A. GOAL

I believe that the fact that the Savior has been born... should be widely made known to the world despite all the ill things that are said about religion.

A

Will these people become aware of it?

R. A. GOAL

It would be OK even if they became aware of it after they go to another world.

A

That would be too late. If we wait until they go to another world before becoming aware of it, it will take them several decades more.

Weekly magazines and YouTube are viruses

R. A. GOAL

Because weekly magazines are viruses.

A

What they are doing is brainwashing people. Their articles contain a lot of prejudice and discrimination against religions.

R. A. GOAL

Yes.

A

They have no right to say that religions brainwash people because the mass media and the Internet are all brainwashing people.

R. A. GOAL

Yes, the Internet and YouTube, they are all viruses.

A

Using fake information without solid evidence.

R. A. GOAL

They are viruses. Aren't they just spreading viruses?

A

Yes.

R. A. GOAL

So they are just like viruses. YouTube is transmitting a lot of bad information one after another. That's a virus, really.

A

I agree they are viruses.

R. A. GOAL

You live in a "virus society," now. That's why these things are becoming popular. If you want to uproot this virus society, it's important not to lie, not to speak ill of others, not to speak ill of God or Buddha, and not to harm devout people.

A

That's absolutely right.

R. A. GOAL

I believe these things are essential and should be the foundation of education. Also, if there arise no problems even when schools are shut down, then what even is the point of education? So I very much feel the shallowness in the way of thinking of the current government.

A

Yes. If we were to say that, they would say that we are to be blamed and that we are doing something crazy.

R. A. GOAL

[*Laughs.*] That may be true. Possibly, the weekly magazine *Bunshun* may leak information to other mass media outlets to have them write articles.

Things to be aware of in this time and age when only bad things are happening

R. A. GOAL

The coronavirus, a global great depression, and swarms of locusts; after these things, there is another one coming. People need to feel that these things are abnormal. They must understand that these are abnormal so that they will realize that divine punishments are unfolding, or that God is furious.

A

Will they realize it?

R. A. GOAL

Who knows?

A

I wonder if they will understand it at this rate.

R. A. GOAL

Well, they may realize it.

A

I see.

R. A. GOAL

Because at least the Abe administration is starting to lose confidence in what they have done.

A

It is beyond human control. That is what brought this about, and the world is on the verge of falling into a worldwide economic recession.

R. A. GOAL

The Reiwa era has created no economic effect whatsoever, right?

A

Right.

R. A. GOAL

Only bad things are happening. This is a bad indication.

A

We know that human beings don't act the way the government expects them to do.

R. A. GOAL

Yes.

A

No matter how far science progresses.

R. A. GOAL

Even if calculations are made.

A

Even if we calculate it, the forecast is...

R. A. GOAL

Statistics is of no help, right?

A

That's right. Forecasts sometimes turn out to be completely wrong.

R. A. GOAL

Yes. But you had better realize that there are many dangerous neighboring countries to the least. They say that an accident occurred at a nuclear power plant in Japan, but you should know that there are countries with these biological weapons and virus weapons, and they actually have missiles of these kinds. We never know when an accident could happen with such weapons, and that such missiles could be launched anytime.

A

I understand.

R. A. GOAL

China is working hard to look for things it can blame on others. North Korea may be the same.

A

The way that China makes statements is really unbelievable. Although it is apparent that the virus outbreak occurred in that country, they say that it is a dishonor to link the coronavirus with China. It's astonishing that they can say this.

R. A. GOAL

China has the desire to conquer the world, but they don't know how to work with the world. So, they are like a gigantic "country bumpkin."

A

They want to rule the world, but they don't feel obliged to take responsibility for it.

R. A. GOAL

China sends off a vast number of Chinese people abroad to buy things in foreign countries and return to the country. It is just like a swarm of flying locusts, or a virus spreading. That's what it signifies.

3

Japan Needs to Rebuild Itself

Now is an opportunity for each country to increase what it can do

R. A. GOAL

Well, please enjoy and look forward to what you will see.

A

"Look forward to what we will see."

R. A. GOAL

I mean, look forward to how things unfold this year. It is an extraordinary experience to witness these things. You should teach people how your Golden Age should open. Some media outlets care about Happy Science and some claim that only Happy Science is pushing hard to hold gatherings.

In the time of Moses, only children with the blood of the Paschal lamb painted on their houses survived, while the children of Egyptians died. At that time, something epidemiologically impossible happened. That was the realm of God. God can do that. God can select. Actually, there have been any numbers of viruses in the air since ancient times. Some get infected, but others don't. When you sterilize the virus too much with fear, the worse results you may face. It's better to think of it as not the virus but just the flu. Not the coronavirus.

A
In a nutshell, there is no drug that is effective on the virus...

R. A. GOAL
They are having trouble.

A
...so people are feeling nervous. That is the problem.

R. A. GOAL
But in reality, no drug works on a new type of influenza.

A

Even the flu drug Tamiflu sometimes causes abnormal symptoms. We are not certain whether an effective and safe drug exists for the flu.

R. A. GOAL

Hmm. You are riding on larger currents of destiny. You can do whatever you think you need to do on the currents. China says that it has already started to break the blockage. This means that people can't stand it anymore. If such a situation continues for more than two months, human beings become insane. Soon...

A

If people are banned from going out for a long period.

R. A. GOAL

Japan will not be able to hold out any longer unless they lift all bans when the new school semester begins (in April). They can't. When you watch the Grand Sumo Tournament on TV and see that there aren't any spectators, you may increasingly feel a sense of depression.

All countries have begun restricting entry by foreigners, and animosity toward foreigners is growing. But this is an opportunity to switch to a style in which each country increases what it can do.

The disaster will last as long as the "Communist virus" exists

R. A. GOAL

Also, your movie, *The Real Exorcist* (Executive producer and original story by Ryuho Okawa, May, 2020) will soon be screened (at the time of recording). There will be a discussion on whether to screen movies, though some are already postponed. The movie last year (*Immortal Hero*, Executive producer Ryuho Okawa, 2019), cured a lot of illnesses, and these two movies will exorcise devils. It's possible to fight off small devils. So, I want people to see the movies to receive light. It's a battle of thoughts. In other words, as long as the Communist virus exists, these disasters will continue.

We are the being that has lived for a long time. We have been watching over humankind for a long time. Please understand that we have the adjustment functions in some places and are thinking about it.

A

Today's Japanese people have ridiculed it.

R. A. GOAL

[*Laughs.*] It's sad for people to have no faith in God.

A

How do they tell good from evil and how do they judge people?

R. A. GOAL

They just think about whether they can make money or not.

A

If so, they have no right to judge people.

R. A. GOAL

At any rate, things will become clear in due course because they make fun of religious rituals.

A

They completely ridicule religion. It appears that they can't tell good religions from bad religions. It's unbelievable. Anyone who thinks about this normally should be able to understand.

R. A. GOAL

It means that Japan needs to rebuild itself. Japan may need a Western-style Angry God. I think so. It's impossible to arrest and condemn me, R. A. Goal.

A

[*Laughs.*]

R. A. GOAL

We are beyond the gods of the Earth, so, unfortunately, that would be impossible.

A

I am sorry. Thank you.

R. A. GOAL

You, Happy Science, should confidently keep going.

A

I understand.

RYUHO OKAWA

Yes [*claps once*].

A

Thank you so much.

It is said from ancient times that those who have attained enlightenment like Shakyamuni Buddha can use abilities beyond human knowledge freely at their will, namely the Six Divine Supernatural Powers (astral travel, clairvoyance, clairaudience, mind-reading, fate-reading, and spiritual wisdom). These spiritual abilities of the highest level transcend the boundaries of time and space, and enable one to freely see through the past, present, and future lives. Okawa is able to use these Six Divine Supernatural Powers freely and conduct various readings.

In the spiritual reading sessions compiled in this book, Okawa uses these abilities to conduct spiritual messages, spiritual vision, time-travel reading (seeing through the subject's past and future), remote-viewing (sending part of the spirit body to a specific location and seeing the situation there), mind-reading (reading the subject's thoughts and will, including those in a remote location), and mutual conversation (communicating with the thoughts of various beings that are beyond human contact).

CHAPTER TWO

Talking about the Savior on a Cosmic Scale beyond the Earth

-UFO Reading 46 (R. A. Goal)-

Originally recorded in Japanese on March 18, 2020,
in the Special Lecture Hall of Happy Science in Japan,
and later translated into English.

The situation when this chapter was recorded

This UFO reading was recorded on March 18, the day after "Warnings of the Pro-China Mentality" (Part Two, Chapter One) was recorded.

1

Thinking about and Dealing with the Novel Coronavirus Infection

Happy Science stands strong against the novel coronavirus infection

RYUHO OKAWA

[*Looks up to the sky.*] The UFO is coming down quite low.

A

I have it on the camera.

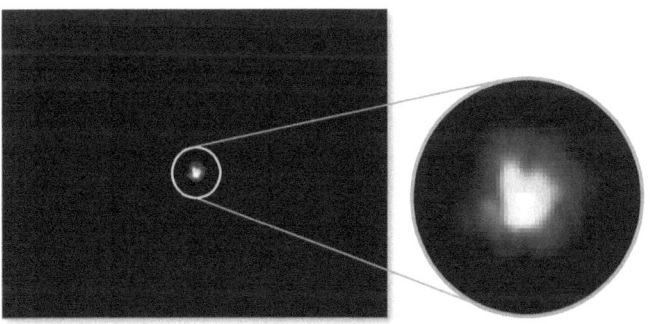

R. A. Goal's UFO captured in this recording session
Spotted by Ryuho Okawa
March 18, 2020, at 10:39 pm in Tokyo
(Right: enlarged image)

* All texts in bold and double quotation marks are the words of the space being that Ryuho Okawa conducted a reading on.

RYUHO OKAWA

OK. The one that seems to be sending a signal, the one that seems to be sending a signal. Who are you?

"R. A. Goal."

A

Thank you very much for yesterday. (See Part Two, Chapter One.)

RYUHO OKAWA

"Sure. I sent a spiritual message, but I didn't send you a visual, so I'm showing us a little."

A

You appeared for us.

RYUHO OKAWA

"We'll be gone after a while."

A

I can see it spinning with the naked eye.

RYUHO OKAWA

"I'm spinning. Yes, that's right."

A

It's shining completely differently from other stars.

RYUHO OKAWA

"Yes, completely different. We're pretty close distance-wise. Not too far."

A

The color is also changing...

RYUHO OKAWA

"Yes, yes. Anyway, I think many people have suffered a shock."

A

Due to the novel coronavirus?

RYUHO OKAWA

"Hmm. I think people are talking about the standpoint of Happy Science or how Happy Science is standing strong and gathering people, and so on. But soon, that's how things will be, otherwise, everything will stop working. China is making a move because they cannot wait any longer.*"

A

Yes.

RYUHO OKAWA

"Yes, that's how it will be."

Japan is behind in information on space people

A

I'm going to move the camera. I locked it.

---

* On April 8, 2020, three weeks after this reading, the Chinese government lifted Wuhan's lockdown.

RYUHO OKAWA

"I heard Japan will be distributing money recklessly again."

A

[*Smiles wryly.*] They will give us cash.

RYUHO OKAWA

"It's like wartime or something."

A

Yes. In that sense, it's crisis management...

RYUHO OKAWA

"Issue."

A

They weren't thinking about crisis management.

RYUHO OKAWA

"Right. The government said they wouldn't raise it (the consumption tax rate) if something like the

Lehman Brothers collapse occurred, but would if it did not. So, they raised it, and now this happened."

A

The color of the UFO is changing a lot.

RYUHO OKAWA

"It's moving, isn't it? It's moving. I'm making it move a lot now. I'm sending you a signal. This is R. A. Goal. I'm sorry for making all of you worry and giving you a hard time."

A

No, no. Thank you for doing so much for us earthlings.

RYUHO OKAWA

"You might lose trust by conveying the opinions of space people, but there are things that only we know."

A

Space people exist. This will surely be common sense in the future.

RYUHO OKAWA

"Yes, of course. Japan had been extremely behind."

A

I'm moving the camera a little.

RYUHO OKAWA

"Happy Science began revealing information about space people over the past decade, so it is being accepted now. Japan had no information on them before that. None. Other countries did, but not Japan. People were saying that maybe Japan was too small for UFOs to appear."

Have a strong mind through faith

A

I'll move the camera a little.

RYUHO OKAWA

"Yes, because we're moving."

A

You're going off the screen a little.

RYUHO OKAWA

"Yes, because we are at a low altitude."

A

I found you. Sorry.

RYUHO OKAWA

"Is there anything you would like to ask?"

A

Yes, please teach us what kind of mindset we should have against the novel coronavirus infection.

RYUHO OKAWA

"OK. Looking at the big picture, you might have a tough time holding large events, but you don't need to stop holding events at branches and shojas (temples), so please go ahead. The leftists might think you are asking for trouble and make a counterattack, but in the end, at times like this, it's

very important for there to be people who carry on calm and composed. Because people don't know what to do. They feel they must really do something. Other countries are also in quite a serious situation. They are closing their borders. But they are all very slow in dealing with this."

A

The UFO is off the screen.

RYUHO OKAWA

"No medicine has been developed for it yet. So, there is no other way than to have a strong mind through faith, as Happy Science says. That's it. That's the countermeasure. We are thinking of other options, in our own way, so please leave it to us."

A

OK. I will zoom in.

RYUHO OKAWA

"At the very least, I want to tell you that, right now, a drastic change is about to happen globally."

A

I'll move the camera. I locked it.

RYUHO OKAWA

"Hmm. China is fighting back so that they are not seen as the evildoer, but we will continue to attack them, more and more. Please keep this in mind. I heard the number of imports from China this February has halved. Japan needs to be able to survive on that or even fewer imports. That's what I want to say. This is extremely important for the future."

Believe in El Cantare—
that is the key to all salvation

RYUHO OKAWA

"You might wonder why space people would care, but we are protecting the Earth. Please understand this and believe us."

A

Disciples of El Cantare in outer space?

RYUHO OKAWA

"Yes, He (El Cantare) will eventually ascend to being a cosmic-scale savior. We came for that purpose. All new things started around 2009 or 2010."

A

I'll lock the camera.

RYUHO OKAWA

"I would like to leave this project as a legacy for future generations."

A

I agree.

RYUHO OKAWA

"Everything started at the same time, you know? Missionary work in Japan and overseas, education projects, and the political party project. Also, the movie project and many more, right?"

A

Yes. I'll zoom in.

RYUHO OKAWA

"It's also important to let them know about space (people)."

It's coming down, so maybe we won't see it anymore.

A

Just a second. But it's still on the screen.

RYUHO OKAWA

"So, please believe us. But in the end, please believe in Happy Science. Believe in Ryuho Okawa. Believe in El Cantare. That's the key to all salvation. Those who believe in the Lord will have eternal life. They will enjoy eternal prosperity."

2

Space People Are Coming to See the Messiah of the Earth

The ongoing battle to overturn mistaken values

A

This spiritual message and messages from outer space are...

RYUHO OKAWA

"Don't be weak."

A

...things that, to tell the truth, we are normally not able to receive this much. Now is a rare time, a miraculous time.

RYUHO OKAWA

"Yes, that's right. We're coming to see you from outer space. That's something that doesn't usually happen. It would normally be impossible."

A

There are very few beings that can convey such words to us.

RYUHO OKAWA

"The only story that remains today is this: when Jesus was born, a star was shining over the stable and three wise men from the East came to see him. That story still remains. The star didn't move, right? That's it, though.

"Now, we're here to see you. We're delivering a message. It's amazing. We're in a battle."

A

Yes. We must be strong-minded, too.

RYUHO OKAWA

"A shift in values. We are trying to overturn mistaken values. Materialists cannot prove that space people do not exist."

A

Right.

RYUHO OKAWA

"So, you must tell the public about it."

A

Actually, many have seen UFOs, but they tend to be blocked from speaking about it.

RYUHO OKAWA

"Yes. That seems to be the case. They think it's classier or more advanced to ignore them."

A

Right.

RYUHO OKAWA

"Well, I'd like to say, 'Please follow us. Don't be weak-minded.' We'll take care of everything in the end."

A

We'll do our best, too. Thank you very much.

RYUHO OKAWA

"We just came to say hello."

The awakening of the Messiah of the Earth is a cosmic-level incident

A

By the way, this is what I was wondering. Master gave lectures at Tokyo Dome in the 1990s, and one of them will be depicted in the movie to be released this fall (*Twiceborn*, executive producer Ryuho Okawa, October, 2020). Were you watching from above at those times?

RYUHO OKAWA
"We were there."

A

I thought so.

RYUHO OKAWA
"We were there, but you weren't looking up at the sky and you didn't record anything. "

A

So, you couldn't appear yet, but you were watching over us in the 90s as well.

RYUHO OKAWA

"We might have seemed to appear when Master began to teach the Laws of the Universe, but we have been in the sky. Of course. The awakening of the Messiah of the Earth is a cosmic-level incident. We need you to be more aware. Also, we will make many things happen to make you more confident."

A

OK. Thank you very much.

RYUHO OKAWA

"OK."

CHAPTER THREE

Awaken to the Faith in the One and Only God

- Spiritual Messages from R. A. Goal -

Originally recorded in Japanese on March 25, 2020,
in the Special Lecture Hall of Happy Science in Japan,
and later translated into English.

The situation when this chapter was recorded

This spiritual message session was recorded on March 25, one week after the spiritual reading (Part Two, Chapter Two) was recorded. At that time, a spiritual interview with the guardian spirit of Manabu Shintani, the head of the *Weekly Bunshun* editorial division, was recorded after Shintani's guardian spirit reacted to Happy Science's publication of *Bunshun no Hodo Rinri wo Tou* (literally, "Questioning the Press Ethics of *Bunshun*") (Tokyo: IRH Press, 2020). Also, *Weekly Shincho* had published an article slandering Happy Science and denying the spiritual, including spiritual messages.

On a different note, on March 26, the U.S. recorded the most number of people infected with the novel coronavirus in the world, surpassing that of China.

1

"Believe in the One and Only God Protecting the Earth"

"Eyes to the mystical world" will open only when you come to believe in God

A

OK.

R. A. GOAL

[*Exhales.*] This is R. A. Goal.

A

We can see you in the night sky.

R. A. GOAL

Japanese weekly magazines, such as *Bunshun* and *Shincho*, are trying to release various articles aimed at spreading materialism, encouraging impiety and attachment to this world. They already mock you for saying that spirits come and speak, but some of them make even more fun of you for saying that you can hear the words of space people, which Japanese people know nothing about.

A

Hearing you say that, it's clear they (weekly magazines) are indeed behind the times.

R. A. GOAL

Yes. What we just want to tell you is that, while we, as representatives, relay all kinds of opinions from outer space, we are not asking you to worship us. I believe it will take much, much longer for human beings on Earth to be able to talk on equal ground with us, who reside in outer space.

The reason we have been working various miracles
In this world, in order to purify it,
Is that we want to tell people
To have faith in the One and Only God.
This is all we ask.
Humankind will become respectable
And their eyes will open to the mystical world

Only when they come to believe in God.
Their mystical eyes for outer space,
For the universe that God has created,
As well as their space brothers that God has created,
Will open for the first time
When they come to believe in God.
Now, we have absolutely no intention
Of proving ourselves
Or asking people to worship us.
Just believe in the One and Only God
Protecting this Earth.
Then, everything will be given to you.

We have revealed a portion of our many activities,
But you might not understand most of them.
However, this is what we can tell you:
If you cannot even believe in
The existence of the Spirit World,
There is no way you can believe in
The existence of God,
And if you cannot believe in
The existence of God,

There is no way you can believe in
The fact that other advanced life-forms
Created by God, in the universe,
Are also undergoing various discipline
As part of their spiritual training.

Now, it seems the world is
In a pandemic caused by the coronavirus,
Showing signs of a worldwide great depression,
And facing many other threats to humankind.
However, they are threats, yet not threats.
What God seeks for is faith.
God wants people to have
The heart to believe in God.
God is just trying to admonish human beings
For their arrogance.

Humble your pride and awaken to faith in God.
At that time, you will know
What "space love" is, the love we have.
El Cantare, Ryuho Okawa, is the only one
Who can convey our voices

To the earthly world now.
He is the only being who can understand
The only true and strong voice of God of the Earth
And our will.

Believe in Lord El Cantare.
Then, you will be able to overcome every crisis
And build a new age in the next century.
Your Golden Age has begun from difficulties.
However, these difficulties are indeed
The crisis necessary to demolish the wrong values
In this world.
It is not a crisis for the sake of a crisis.
We are not doing this to bully you, either.
We just want you to awaken to the true faith.

This (pandemic) will be explained
In various ways.
But sometimes,
People realize their arrogance for the first time,
Only when something unprecedented happens
That makes them face problems

Which cannot be solved by their knowledge.

We want them to realize that

They are powerless.

At that time, they will need someone

Who conveys the words of God.

Such a person is living in this world.

This fact, itself, is salvation.

Please know this.

"You cannot get true faith if you are swayed by words of secular people"

R. A. GOAL

I call myself "R. A. Goal,"

But you do not need to worship me.

Please think that

This is a voice from somewhere in the universe.

We just want to tell you that

The Earth is being targeted by evil forces.

So, please spread these words:

"The one and only faith is faith in El Cantare."

You will resist the crowds of disbelievers

Using every means possible.

I hope so.

A

I understand. Our spiritual messages started more than 30 years ago.

R. A. GOAL

Yes.

A

So, why bring it up now?

R. A. GOAL

I agree. Some people try to stir up disbelief by exaggerating small issues, but please do not forget that there were such small-minded people in every age.

A

Yes. I'm sick of what the Japanese weekly magazines are saying.

R. A. GOAL

Right.

> You can never get true faith
>
> If you are swayed by such words of
>
> Impious or secular people.
>
> Believe in your Lord God.
>
> The Lord God is connected to the universe.
>
> You cannot learn the true view of the universe
>
> Except through the One and Only God.
>
> Please live powerfully
>
> And with a strong mind.

A

Yes, we will do our best. We will never lose.

R. A. GOAL

OK.

2

Don't Be Defeated by Lies or Traps in This World, and Be Strong

Chinese lies and aims involving the novel coronavirus

A

I have a question. Right now, the Chinese government is claiming that the coronavirus was brought into China by the U.S. They are also saying that the number of infected is decreasing and that the infection stopped spreading. I've heard that the infection is spreading in the U.S., which will be the next region to suffer an outbreak. What do you think of that?

R. A. GOAL

They are lying. The number of infected is not declining in China. How can the infection stop when they have neither a vaccine nor a treatment? They are just reducing it in terms of statistics. That's all.

A

The guardian spirit of Xi Jinping also said that the economy will recover if the government says that the infection has passed its peak.

R. A. GOAL

He must be hoping so. But what the Chinese government is hiding will come to light once again. The numbers reported by the U.S. must be accurate, so the U.S. will have to fight against China to the end. The U.S. will likely fight using modern means, but you should know that there might be someone plotting to make the world think that it was the Americans who spread the infection. Someone could be thinking like that.

The Chinese government's aim is to sway people's faith in Christianity, the Vatican, and also to sway America's self-esteem as the nation of God. They want to show that a materialistic nation is strong. However, their lies will be revealed soon.

The Chinese government claims that they have succeeded in containing the infection so that they can get the support of pro-Chinese, simple-minded people in Japan, but unfortunately, China has no hospitals, doctors, medicine, or facilities to contain the infection. They have nothing. Therefore, the scary thing is that people in China can be wiped out if they show symptoms.

Egotistic people easily walk into traps called "desires"

A

What is interesting, from a larger perspective, is that the world is fighting against such a lying nation. Happy Science is also fighting against liars. Devils and bad people lie.

R. A. GOAL

That's right.

A

People become liars when they are possessed by evil spirits.

R. A. GOAL

Devils are trying to satisfy people's desires. Devils say, "If you listen to us, you will obtain everything you desire, including conquest, control, power, possessions, and sex.

You will be happy. We are the true gods." They spread these lies. So, of course, Happy Science will clash with such groups.

A

They will do whatever it takes to get what they want.

R. A. GOAL

Yes.

A

So, they lie.

R. A. GOAL

God and His agents teach you to abandon desires, follow precepts, and limit your freedom and be responsible, which are all extremely boring for devils. Countless people fall into such simple traps by devils. This world is full of traps. Egotistic people easily walk into traps. They fall into a pit; a pit named "desire." This is a classical trap. It's a very classical trap in the world of religion.

A

In a nutshell, they are liars. It's surprising they can be summed up like that.

R. A. GOAL

It is the same as animal traps. Just dig a hole and cover it with grass, then someone who walks on it will fall. That's it.

A

And leave some bait.

R. A. GOAL

Yes.

A

I understand.

"Don't lose" "Be strong"

R. A. GOAL

Do not lose. Don't fall for such a classical trap. Be strong.

A

We will.

R. A. GOAL

More and more people are coming to believe in Happy Science. The number of people who believe in you is increasing higher than the number of readers of weekly magazines.

A

Weekly magazines will fall behind the times.

R. A. GOAL

Yes. Please know that you are now spreading opinions as the center of the Earth. It seems our fellow space people have gathered around during this session.

A

Oh, is that so? Thank you very much.

R. A. GOAL

Two, three, or four have come. But anyway, we are just supporting you. We are lending you power from behind, but please establish faith by yourselves, the Earthlings. That is the important thing.

A

Yes.

R. A. GOAL

Even so, we will protect you when you are in danger.

A

We are really grateful.

R. A. GOAL

Yes.

A

Yes, thank you very much.

Afterword

This is a strict view of the Japanese. It should be shocking for Japanese people who are losing their faith and have very little interest in outer space.

The Japanese mass media are very much behind, and it seems they have become "mass trash." Also, the comment that YouTube and the Internet are like a virus infection has left an impression on me.

The current "coronavirus pandemic" is closely related to Chinese hegemony. It is on this that the two spirits base their claim.

We are now at a crossroads to the future. The coronavirus is taking away the lives of the generation who were strongly attracted to China and campaigned against the Japan-U.S. Security Treaty, and who lived through the Cold War. "Ignorance" is a serious sin, indeed.

The current Japanese government, which is only thinking about scattering ¥100,000 to each person, will soon be judged. The time of wishful thinking has already ended.

Ryuho Okawa
Master & CEO of Happy Science Group
April 21, 2020

ABOUT THE AUTHOR

Founder and CEO of Happy Science Group.

Ryuho Okawa was born on July 7th 1956, in Tokushima, Japan. After graduating from the University of Tokyo with a law degree, he joined a Tokyo-based trading house. While working at its New York headquarters, he studied international finance at the Graduate Center of the City University of New York. In 1981, he attained Great Enlightenment and became aware that he is El Cantare with a mission to bring salvation to all humankind.

In 1986, he established Happy Science. It now has members in over 165 countries across the world, with more than 700 branches and temples as well as 10,000 missionary houses around the world.

He has given over 3,450 lectures (of which more than 150 are in English) and published over 3,000 books (of which more than 600 are Spiritual Interview Series), and many are translated into 40 languages. Along with *The Laws of the Sun* and *The Laws Of Messiah*, many of the books have become best sellers or million sellers. To date, Happy Science has produced 25 movies. The original story and original concept were given by the Executive Producer Ryuho Okawa. He has also composed music and written lyrics of over 450 pieces.

Moreover, he is the Founder of Happy Science University and Happy Science Academy (Junior and Senior High School), Founder and President of the Happiness Realization Party, Founder and Honorary Headmaster of Happy Science Institute of Government and Management, Founder of IRH Press Co., Ltd., and the Chairperson of NEW STAR PRODUCTION Co., Ltd. and ARI Production Co., Ltd.

WHAT IS EL CANTARE?

El Cantare means "the Light of the Earth," and is the Supreme God of the Earth who has been guiding humankind since the beginning of Genesis. He is whom Jesus called Father and Muhammad called Allah, and is *Ame-no-Mioya-Gami*, Japanese Father God. Different parts of El Cantare's core consciousness have descended to Earth in the past, once as Alpha and another as Elohim. His branch spirits, such as Shakyamuni Buddha and Hermes, have descended to Earth many times and helped to flourish many civilizations. To unite various religions and to integrate various fields of study in order to build a new civilization on Earth, a part of the core consciousness has descended to Earth as Master Ryuho Okawa.

Alpha is a part of the core consciousness of El Cantare who descended to Earth around 330 million years ago. Alpha preached Earth's Truths to harmonize and unify Earth-born humans and space people who came from other planets.

Elohim is a part of El Cantare's core consciousness who descended to Earth around 150 million years ago. He gave wisdom, mainly on the differences of light and darkness, good and evil.

Ame-no-Mioya-Gami (Japanese Father God) is the Creator God and the Father God who appears in the ancient literature, *Hotsuma Tsutae*. It is believed that He descended on the foothills of Mt. Fuji about 30,000 years ago and built the Fuji dynasty, which is the root of the Japanese civilization. With justice as the central pillar, Ame-no-Mioya-Gami's teachings spread to ancient civilizations of other countries in the world.

Shakyamuni Buddha was born as a prince into the Shakya Clan in India around 2,600 years ago. When he was 29 years old, he renounced the world and sought enlightenment. He later attained Great Enlightenment and founded Buddhism.

Hermes is one of the 12 Olympian gods in Greek mythology, but the spiritual Truth is that he taught the teachings of love and progress around 4,300 years ago that became the origin of the current Western civilization. He is a hero that truly existed.

Ophealis was born in Greece around 6,500 years ago and was the leader who took an expedition to as far as Egypt. He is the God of miracles, prosperity, and arts, and is known as Osiris in the Egyptian mythology.

Rient Arl Croud was born as a king of the ancient Incan Empire around 7,000 years ago and taught about the mysteries of the mind. In the heavenly world, he is responsible for the interactions that take place between various planets.

Thoth was an almighty leader who built the golden age of the Atlantic civilization around 12,000 years ago. In the Egyptian mythology, he is known as god Thoth.

Ra Mu was a leader who built the golden age of the civilization of Mu around 17,000 years ago. As a religious leader and a politician, he ruled by uniting religion and politics.

WHAT IS A SPIRITUAL MESSAGE?

We are all spiritual beings living on this earth. The following is the mechanism behind Master Ryuho Okawa's spiritual messages.

1 You are a spirit

People are born into this world to gain wisdom through various experiences and return to the other world when their lives end. We are all spirits and repeat this cycle in order to refine our souls.

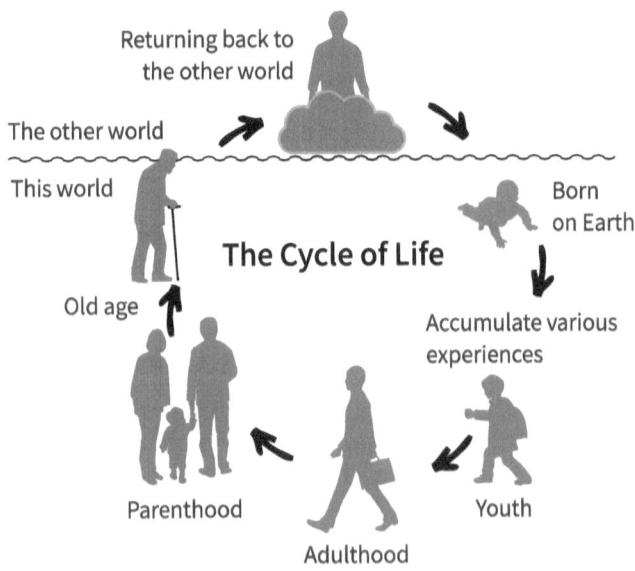

2 You have a guardian spirit

Guardian spirits are those who protect the people who are living on this earth. Each of us has a guardian spirit that watches over us and guides us from the other world. They were us in our past life, and are identical in how we think.

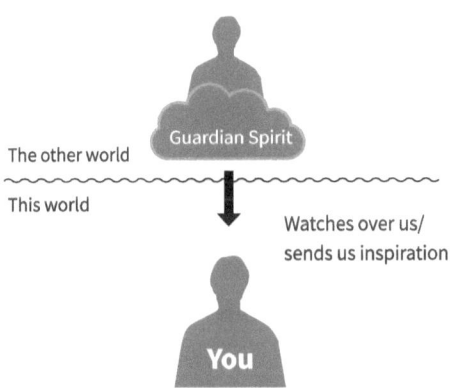

The other world

This world

Guardian Spirit

Watches over us/ sends us inspiration

You

3 How spiritual messages work

Master Ryuho Okawa, through his enlightenment, is capable of summoning any spirit from anywhere in the world, including the spirit world.

Master Okawa's way of receiving spiritual messages is fundamentally different from that of other psychic mediums who undergo trances and are thereby completely taken over by the spirits they are channeling.

Master Okawa's attainment of a high level of enlightenment enables him to retain full control of his consciousness and body throughout the duration of the spiritual message. To allow the spirits to express their own thoughts and personalities freely, however, Master Okawa usually softens the dominancy of his consciousness. This way, he is able to keep his own philosophies out of the way and ensure that the spiritual messages are pure expressions of the spirits he is channeling.

Since guardian spirits think at the same subconscious level as the person living on earth, Master Okawa can summon the spirit and find out what the person on earth is actually thinking. If the person has already returned to the other world, the spirit can give messages to the people living on earth through Master Okawa.

Since 2009, many spiritual messages have been openly recorded by Master Okawa and published. Spiritual messages from the guardian spirits of people living today such as Donald Trump, former Japanese Prime Minister Shinzo Abe and Chinese President Xi Jinping, as well as spiritual messages sent from the spirit world by Jesus Christ, Muhammad, Thomas Edison, Mother Teresa, Steve Jobs and Nelson Mandela are just a tiny pack of spiritual messages that were published so far.

Domestically, in Japan, these spiritual messages are being read by a wide range of politicians and mass media, and the high-level contents of these books are delivering an impact even more on politics, news and public opinion. In recent years, there have been spiritual messages recorded in English, and

English translations are being done on the spiritual messages given in Japanese. These have been published overseas, one after another, and have started to shake the world.

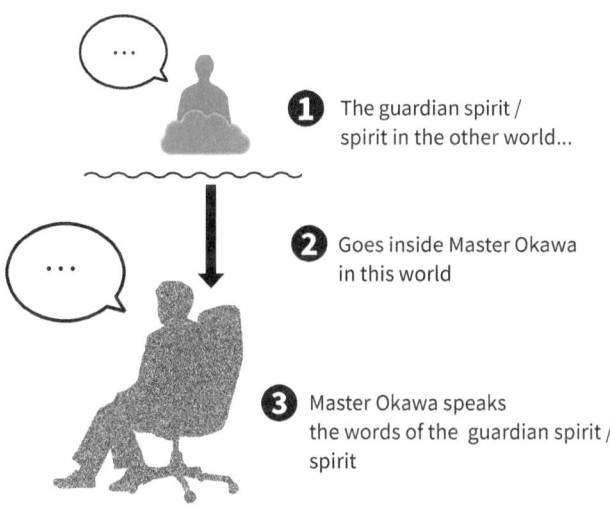

1. The guardian spirit / spirit in the other world...

2. Goes inside Master Okawa in this world

3. Master Okawa speaks the words of the guardian spirit / spirit

For more about spiritual messages and a complete list of books in the Spiritual Interview Series, visit okawabooks.com

ABOUT HAPPY SCIENCE

Happy Science is a global movement that empowers individuals to find purpose and spiritual happiness and to share that happiness with their families, societies, and the world. With more than 12 million members around the world, Happy Science aims to increase awareness of spiritual truths and expand our capacity for love, compassion, and joy so that together we can create the kind of world we all wish to live in.

Activities at Happy Science are based on the Principle of Happiness (Love, Wisdom, Self-Reflection, and Progress). This principle embraces worldwide philosophies and beliefs, transcending boundaries of culture and religions.

Love teaches us to give ourselves freely without expecting anything in return; it encompasses giving, nurturing, and forgiving.

Wisdom leads us to the insights of spiritual truths, and opens us to the true meaning of life and the will of God (the universe, the highest power, Buddha).

Self-Reflection brings a mindful, nonjudgmental lens to our thoughts and actions to help us find our truest selves—the essence of our souls—and deepen our connection to the highest power. It helps us attain a clean and peaceful mind and leads us to the right life path.

Progress emphasizes the positive, dynamic aspects of our spiritual growth—actions we can take to manifest and spread happiness around the world. It's a path that not only expands our soul growth, but also furthers the collective potential of the world we live in.

PROGRAMS AND EVENTS

The doors of Happy Science are open to all. We offer a variety of programs and events, including self-exploration and self-growth programs, spiritual seminars, meditation and contemplation sessions, study groups, and book events.

Our programs are designed to:
* Deepen your understanding of your purpose and meaning in life
* Improve your relationships and increase your capacity to love unconditionally
* Attain peace of mind, decrease anxiety and stress, and feel positive
* Gain deeper insights and a broader perspective on the world
* Learn how to overcome life's challenges
  ... and much more.

For more information, visit _happy-science.org_.

OUR ACTIVITIES

Happy Science does other various activities to provide support for those in need.

◆ **You Are An Angel! General Incorporated Association**

Happy Science has a volunteer network in Japan that encourages and supports children with disabilities as well as their parents and guardians.

◆ **Never Mind School for Truancy**

At 'Never Mind,' we support students who find it very challenging to attend schools in Japan. We also nurture their self-help spirit and power to rebound against obstacles in life based on Master Okawa's teachings and faith.

◆ **"Prevention Against Suicide" Campaign since 2003**

A nationwide campaign to reduce suicides; over 20,000 people commit suicide every year in Japan. "The Suicide Prevention Website-Words of Truth for You-" presents spiritual prescriptions for worries such as depression, lost love, extramarital affairs, bullying and work-related problems, thereby saving many lives.

◆ **Support for Anti-bullying Campaigns**

Happy Science provides support for a group of parents and guardians, Network to Protect Children from Bullying, a general incorporated foundation launched in Japan to end bullying, including those that can even be called a criminal offense. So far, the network received more than 5,000 cases and resolved 90% of them.

- **The Golden Age Scholarship**

  This scholarship is granted to students who can contribute greatly and bring a hopeful future to the world.

- **Success No.1**
  Buddha's Truth Afterschool Academy

  Happy Science has over 180 classrooms throughout Japan and in several cities around the world that focus on afterschool education for children. The education focuses on faith and morals in addition to supporting children's school studies.

- **Angel Plan V**

  For children under the age of kindergarten, Happy Science holds classes for nurturing healthy, positive, and creative boys and girls.

- **Future Stars Training Department**

  The Future Stars Training Department was founded within the Happy Science Media Division with the goal of nurturing talented individuals to become successful in the performing arts and entertainment industry.

- **NEW STAR PRODUCTION Co., Ltd.**
  ARI Production Co., Ltd.

  We have companies to nurture actors and actresses, artists, and vocalists. They are also involved in film production.

CONTACT INFORMATION

Happy Science is a worldwide organization with branches and temples around the globe. For a comprehensive list, visit the worldwide directory at *happy-science.org*. The following are some of the many Happy Science locations:

UNITED STATES AND CANADA

New York
79 Franklin St., New York, NY 10013, USA
Phone: 1-212-343-7972
Fax: 1-212-343-7973
Email: ny@happy-science.org
Website: happyscience-usa.org

New Jersey
66 Hudson St., #2R, Hoboken, NJ 07030, USA
Phone: 1-201-313-0127
Email: nj@happy-science.org
Website: happyscience-usa.org

Chicago
2300 Barrington Rd., Suite #400,
Hoffman Estates, IL 60169, USA
Phone: 1-630-937-3077
Email: chicago@happy-science.org
Website: happyscience-usa.org

Florida
5208 8th St., Zephyrhills, FL 33542, USA
Phone: 1-813-715-0000
Fax: 1-813-715-0010
Email: florida@happy-science.org
Website: happyscience-usa.org

Atlanta
1874 Piedmont Ave., NE Suite 360-C
Atlanta, GA 30324, USA
Phone: 1-404-892-7770
Email: atlanta@happy-science.org
Website: happyscience-usa.org

San Francisco
525 Clinton St.
Redwood City, CA 94062, USA
Phone & Fax: 1-650-363-2777
Email: sf@happy-science.org
Website: happyscience-usa.org

Los Angeles
1590 E. Del Mar Blvd., Pasadena, CA
91106, USA
Phone: 1-626-395-7775
Fax: 1-626-395-7776
Email: la@happy-science.org
Website: happyscience-usa.org

Orange County
16541 Gothard St. Suite 104
Huntington Beach, CA 92647
Phone: 1-714-659-1501
Email: oc@happy-science.org
Website: happyscience-usa.org

San Diego
7841 Balboa Ave. Suite #202
San Diego, CA 92111, USA
Phone: 1-626-395-7775
Fax: 1-626-395-7776
E-mail: sandiego@happy-science.org
Website: happyscience-usa.org

Hawaii
Phone: 1-808-591-9772
Fax: 1-808-591-9776
Email: hi@happy-science.org
Website: happyscience-usa.org

Kauai
3343 Kanakolu Street, Suite 5
Lihue, HI 96766, USA
Phone: 1-808-822-7007
Fax: 1-808-822-6007
Email: kauai-hi@happy-science.org
Website: happyscience-usa.org

Toronto

845 The Queensway
Etobicoke, ON M8Z 1N6, Canada
Phone: 1-416-901-3747
Email: toronto@happy-science.org
Website: happy-science.ca

Vancouver

#201-2607 East 49th Avenue,
Vancouver, BC, V5S 1J9, Canada
Phone: 1-604-437-7735
Fax: 1-604-437-7764
Email: vancouver@happy-science.org
Website: happy-science.ca

INTERNATIONAL

Tokyo

1-6-7 Togoshi, Shinagawa,
Tokyo, 142-0041, Japan
Phone: 81-3-6384-5770
Fax: 81-3-6384-5776
Email: tokyo@happy-science.org
Website: happy-science.org

Seoul

74, Sadang-ro 27-gil,
Dongjak-gu, Seoul, Korea
Phone: 82-2-3478-8777
Fax: 82-2-3478-9777
Email: korea@happy-science.org
Website: happyscience-korea.org

London

3 Margaret St.
London, W1W 8RE United Kingdom
Phone: 44-20-7323-9255
Fax: 44-20-7323-9344
Email: eu@happy-science.org
Website: www.happyscience-uk.org

Taipei

No. 89, Lane 155, Dunhua N. Road,
Songshan District, Taipei City 105, Taiwan
Phone: 886-2-2719-9377
Fax: 886-2-2719-5570
Email: taiwan@happy-science.org
Website: happyscience-tw.org

Sydney

516 Pacific Highway, Lane Cove North,
2066 NSW, Australia
Phone: 61-2-9411-2877
Fax: 61-2-9411-2822
Email: sydney@happy-science.org

Kuala Lumpur

No 22A, Block 2, Jalil Link Jalan Jalil
Jaya 2, Bukit Jalil 57000,
Kuala Lumpur, Malaysia
Phone: 60-3-8998-7877
Fax: 60-3-8998-7977
Email: malaysia@happy-science.org
Website: happyscience.org.my

Sao Paulo

Rua. Domingos de Morais 1154,
Vila Mariana, Sao Paulo SP
CEP 04010-100, Brazil
Phone: 55-11-5088-3800
Email: sp@happy-science.org
Website: happyscience.com.br

Kathmandu

Kathmandu Metropolitan City,
Ward No. 15, Ring Road, Kimdol,
Sitapaila Kathmandu, Nepal
Phone: 977-1-427-2931
Email: nepal@happy-science.org

Jundiai

Rua Congo, 447, Jd. Bonfiglioli
Jundiai-CEP, 13207-340, Brazil
Phone: 55-11-4587-5952
Email: jundiai@happy-science.org

Kampala

Plot 877 Rubaga Road, Kampala
P.O. Box 34130 Kampala, UGANDA
Phone: 256-79-4682-121
Email: uganda@happy-science.org

# ABOUT HAPPINESS REALIZATION PARTY

The Happiness Realization Party (HRP) was founded in May 2009 by Master Ryuho Okawa as part of the Happy Science Group. HRP strives to improve the Japanese society, based on three basic political principles of "freedom, democracy, and faith," and let Japan promote individual and public happiness from Asia to the world as a leader nation.

1) Diplomacy and Security: Protecting Freedom, Democracy, and Faith of Japan and the World from China's Totalitarianism

Japan's current defense system is insufficient against China's expanding hegemony and the threat of North Korea's nuclear missiles. Japan, as the leader of Asia, must strengthen its defense power and promote strategic diplomacy together with the nations which share the values of freedom, democracy, and faith. Further, HRP aims to realize world peace under the leadership of Japan, the nation with the spirit of religious tolerance.

2) Economy: Early economic recovery through utilizing the "wisdom of the private sector"

Economy has been damaged severely by the novel coronavirus originated in China. Many companies have been forced into bankruptcy or out of business. What is needed for economic recovery now is not subsidies and regulations by the government, but policies which can utilize the "wisdom of the private sector."

For more information, visit en.hr-party.jp

ABOUT HS PRESS

HS Press is an imprint of IRH Press Co., Ltd. IRH Press Co., Ltd., based in Tokyo, was founded in 1987 as a publishing division of Happy Science. IRH Press publishes religious and spiritual books, journals, magazines and also operates broadcast and film production enterprises. For more information, visit *okawabooks.com*.

Follow us on:

f Facebook: Okawa Books   ⊙ Instagram: OkawaBooks

▶ Youtube: Okawa Books   🐦 Twitter: Okawa Books

𝓟 Pinterest: Okawa Books   g Goodreads: Ryuho Okawa

——— **NEWSLETTER** ———

To receive book related news, promotions and events, please subscribe to our newsletter below.

∞ eepurl.com/bsMeJj

——— **AUDIO / VISUAL MEDIA** ———

YOUTUBE   **PODCAST**

Introduction of Ryuho Okawa's titles; topics ranging from self-help, current affairs, spirituality, religion, and the universe.

BOOKS BY RYUHO OKAWA

THE LAWS OF STEEL
LIVING A LIFE OF RESILIENCE, CONFIDENCE AND PROSPERITY

Paperback • 256 pages • $16.95
ISBN: 978-1-942125-65-5

This book is a compilation of six lectures that Ryuho Okawa gave in 2018 and 2019, each containing passionate messages for us to open a brighter future. This powerful and inspiring book will not only show us the ways to achieve true happiness and prosperity, but also the ways to solve many global issues we now face. It presents us with wisdom that is based on a spiritual perspective, and a new design for our future society. Through this book, we can overcome different values and create a peaceful world, thereby ushering in a Golden Age.

THE LAWS OF THE SUN
ONE SOURCE, ONE PLANET, ONE PEOPLE

Paperback • 288 pages • $15.95
ISBN: 978-1-942125-43-3

Imagine if you could ask God why he created this world and what spiritual laws he used to shape us—and everything around us. In *The Laws of the Sun*, Ryuho Okawa outlines these laws of the universe and provides a road map for living one's life with greater purpose and meaning. This powerful book shows the way to realize true happiness—a happiness that continues from this world through the other.

For a complete list of books, visit okawabooks.com

THE GOLDEN LAWS

HISTORY THROUGH THE EYES OF THE ETERNAL BUDDHA

Paperback • 201 pages • $14.95
ISBN: 978-1-941779-81-1

Throughout history, Great Guiding Spirits of Light have been present on Earth in both the East and the West at crucial points in human history to further our spiritual development. *The Golden Laws* reveals how Divine Plan has been unfolding on Earth, and outlines 5,000 years of the secret history of humankind. Once we understand the true course of history, through past, present and into the future, we cannot help but become aware of the significance of our spiritual mission in the present age.

THE NINE DIMENSIONS

UNVEILING THE LAWS OF ETERNITY

Paperback • 168 pages • $15.95
ISBN: 978-0-982698-56-3

This book is a window into the mind of our loving God, who designed this world and the vast, wondrous world of our afterlife as a school with many levels through which our souls learn and grow. When the religions and cultures of the world discover the truth of their common spiritual origin, they will be inspired to accept their differences, come together under faith in God, and build an era of harmony and peaceful progress on Earth.

For a complete list of books, visit okawabooks.com

THE REAL EXORCIST
ATTAIN WISDOM TO CONQUER EVIL

Paperback • 208 pages • $16.95
ISBN:978-1-942125-67-9

This is a profound spiritual text backed by the author's nearly 40 years of real-life experience with spiritual phenomena. In it, Okawa teaches how we may discern and overcome our negative tendencies, by acquiring the right knowledge, mindset and lifestyle.

JESUS CHRIST'S ANSWERS TO THE CORONAVIRUS PANDEMIC

Paperback • 204 pages • $11.95
ISBN: 978-1-943869-81-7

In this book, the spirit of Jesus answers the causes, prospects, and coping strategies for the novel coronavirus pandemic. Instead of hoping for the development of an effective vaccine to come soon, we should use our spiritual power to defeat the evil thoughts that spiritually possess this virus. It's a book for all who believe in Jesus.

WHAT WILL BECOME OF CORONAVIRUS PANDEMIC?
READINGS BY EDGAR CAYCE

Paperback • 86 pages • $9.95
ISBN: 978-1-943869-82-4

Edgar Cayce, now a spirit in heaven, tells us that the novel coronavirus infection is likely to spread even further, but he also teaches us the truth behind it and how to deal with it. But you, yourself, can gain the power to defeat the novel coronavirus. Here is your light of hope.

For a complete list of books, visit okawabooks.com

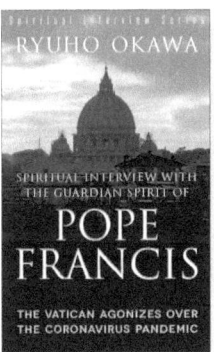

SPIRITUAL INTERVIEW WITH THE GUARDIAN SPIRIT OF POPE FRANCIS

THE VATICAN AGONIZES OVER THE CORONAVIRUS PANDEMIC

Paperback • 268 pages • $13.95
ISBN: 978-1-943869-84-8

In this book, the guardian spirit of Pope Francis confesses his hopelessness, goodwill, and limit as a human being amid the ongoing coronavirus pandemic. Are his prayers heard by Jesus? By also reading *Jesus Christ's Answers to the Coronavirus Pandemic*, you will be able to understand the true will of Jesus and the faith in true God.

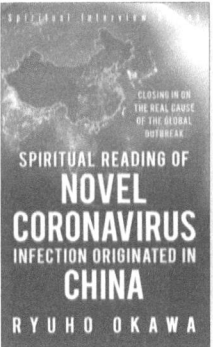

SPIRITUAL READING OF NOVEL CORONAVIRUS INFECTION ORIGINATED IN CHINA

CLOSING IN ON THE REAL CAUSE OF THE GLOBAL OUTBREAK

Paperback • 278 pages • $13.95
ISBN: 978-1-943869-77-0

This worldwide pandemic is not a mere act of nature nor a coincidence, but rather, heaven's warning to humanity, especially China. Through this book, you can find out "the immunity" against the novel coronavirus, among other shocking truths.

UFOS CAUGHT ON CAMERA!

A SPIRITUAL INVESTIGATION ON VIDEOS AND PHOTOS OF THE LUMINOUS OBJECTS VISITING EARTH

Paperback • 112 pages • $17.95
ISBN: 978-1-943869-31-2

In the Summer of 2018, over 60 types of UFOs appeared before the author. *UFOs Caught on Camera!* is a detailed compilation of Okawa's sightings, with visual analysis of the luminous objects visiting Earth and spiritually sourced commentary of the extraterrestrial intelligence behind them.

For a complete list of books, visit okawabooks.com

THE NEW RESURRECTION
My Miraculous Story of Overcoming Illness and Death

THE ROYAL ROAD OF LIFE
Beginning Your Path of Inner Peace, Virtue, and a Life of Purpose

THE LAWS OF GREAT ENLIGHTENMENT
Always Walk with Buddha

I CAN
Discover Your Power Within

THE HELL YOU NEVER KNEW
And How to Avoid Going There

THE LAWS OF FAITH
One World Beyond Differences

THE STARTING POINT OF HAPPINESS
An Inspiring Guide to Positive Living with Faith, Love,
and Courage

HEALING FROM WITHIN
Life-Changing Keys to Calm, Spiritual, and Healthy Living

SPIRITUAL WORLD 101
A Guide to a Spiritually Happy Life

For a complete list of books, visit okawabooks.com

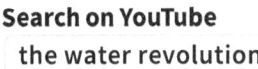

With Savior *English version*

This is the message of hope to the modern people who are living in the midst of the Coronavirus pandemic, natural disasters, economic depression, and other various crises.

Search on YouTube

with savior 🔍 for a short ad!

The Thunder
a composition for repelling the Coronavirus

We have been granted this music from our Lord. It will repel away the novel Coronavirus originated in China. Experience this magnificent powerful music.

Search on YouTube

the thunder composition 🔍

for a short ad!

The Exorcism
prayer music for repelling Lost Spirits

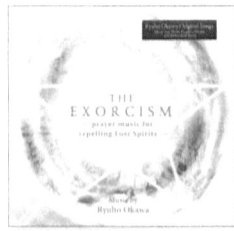

Feel the divine vibrations of this Japanese and Western exorcising symphony to banish all evil possessions you suffer from and to purify your space!

Search on YouTube

the exorcism repelling 🔍

for a short ad!

Listen now today!